A GUIDE TO TH
OF BRIGHTON

School of Architecture and Interior Desi
Brighton Polytechnic

This guide has been written by students a ... t from the John and Heather Lomax Student Pr ... nstitute of British Architects.

It sets out to identify a cross section of interesting buildings which can be seen in and around Brighton. Buildings have been chosen for any one of several reasons: they may be buildings of outstanding architectural quality or buildings of historic importance; they may typify a particular type of building or a particular period. In some cases they may be buildings of little or no merit whose prominent position makes it difficult for them to be passed over!

Brighton is an attractive town enjoying a warm climate and a beautiful situation. It can boast a fine inheritance of marvellous buildings, particularly from the late Georgian and early Victorian periods. Some quite terrible things have happened to the town during recent years: fine buildings have been needlessly destroyed and ugly buildings have appeared in their place. However, the guide is intended primarily to be a celebration, and the temptation to hurl the occasional brickbat has almost always been resisted.

The area covered by the guide stretches from Shoreham in the west to Saltdean in the east. It had been intended to use the South Downs as the northern boundary, but the strong historic and cultural ties which link the town of Lewes to Brighton argued for its inclusion. In particular it was felt that Lewes could offer the visitor glimpses of building styles and methods of construction which had once existed in Brighton but which had been obliterated by 18th century developments.

HOW TO USE THIS GUIDE

The main part of the guide has been divided into 18 sections, corresponding to 18 separate geographic areas. Each section is preceded by a map and a short introductory paragraph. Within each section buildings are described wherever possible in a sequence which corresponds to a suggested promenade. Buildings are given a code which consists of a number followed by a capital letter. The number refers to the section, and the letter identifies the building within its section. Thus 7E is the code for the Royal Crescent: it appears as an entry in Section 7 which covers the Eastern Seafront. The same code is used to locate the Royal Crescent on the map at the beginning of Section 7, and to identify any illustrations which relate to the Royal Crescent.

A general map inside the front and back covers acts as a key to the 18 section maps.

The guide proper begins with the Pavilion Estate which occupies the very heart of Brighton before moving gradually outwards towards the periphery to arrive finally at Lewes and Shoreham. The 'Seaside' has been treated separately from the 'Seafront', while the 'Seafront' is split into two by its encounter with the Steine. The political boundary between Hove and Brighton corresponds neither to an environmental nor an architectural break, and the section on Hove stretches no further east than Grand Avenue.

Three short essays serve as a general introduction. The first of these traces the history of Brighton's development from its origins as a fishing and farming community, through its transformation into a fashionable resort to its final emergence as a commercial and business centre. The second attempts to evaluate the legacy of Amon Wilds, Amon Henry Wilds and Charles Busby who, working together and separately as architects and developers, had such an important impact on Brighton during the late Georgian and early Victorian periods. The third looks at the lives of Henry Michell Wagner and his son Arthur Douglas Wagner and at the wave of church building over which they presided during the Victorian period.

LIST OF CONTENTS

THE DEVELOPMENT OF BRIGHTON

Brighton has been one of Britain's major seaside resorts since the end of the 18th century. Its rapid growth from that time had important consequences for the surrounding region and influenced the emergence of Hove and Worthing as major residential resorts and the development of large coastal dormitories such as those at Saltdean and Peacehaven. In its heyday it was a leader of taste and fashion and its name has become almost synonymous with the Regency Style. Today Brighton and Hove together form the main urban centre in the south-east corner of England outside of the London conurbation. They act as a service centre to a region, eclipsing Chichester and Lewes, the county towns of the two halves of Sussex, and remain important as resorts for long-term residents, day-trippers, and for the conference industry. The persistent demand for housing of one sort or another has resulted in a continuous urban development which stretches between the Downs and the English Channel from Peacehaven in the east to Shoreham in the west.

Beginnings

Little is known about the early history of Brighton before the beginning of the 16th century. The scant surviving evidence suggests that it was a small agricultural and fishing community called Brighthelmstone, more important than neighbouring downland villages such as Preston and Patcham, but totally eclipsed by the town of Lewes 11 miles away to the north-east. At the beginning of the 16th century the upper town was located on a low cliff to the west of the Steine and consisted of three principal streets arranged around the three sides of the Hempshares, a rectangular open space facing the sea. A market place stood at the cliff's edge and nearby a group of buildings formed the beginnings of Ship Street and Black Lion Street, both of them named after inns. Paths led down the cliffs to the broad beach which was a unique feature on this stretch of the coast. Here stood a collection of cottages surrounded by narrow wooden net houses, herring houses and the large capstans which were used to haul the boats out of the English Channel and onto the beach.

The town was surrounded by its own farmlands which occupied the rest of the parish. The arable land was divided into 5 enormous fields called "laines" which were sub-divided into strips called "paulpieces". In theory the land was cultivated under the common field system whereby each farmer was allocated strips of land in various of the laines, but in practice by the late 16th century most of the land was owned by a few people and cultivated by a declining number of tenant farmers. The arable land was used to produce grain, and large flocks of sheep were kept on the downland beyond it. The common field

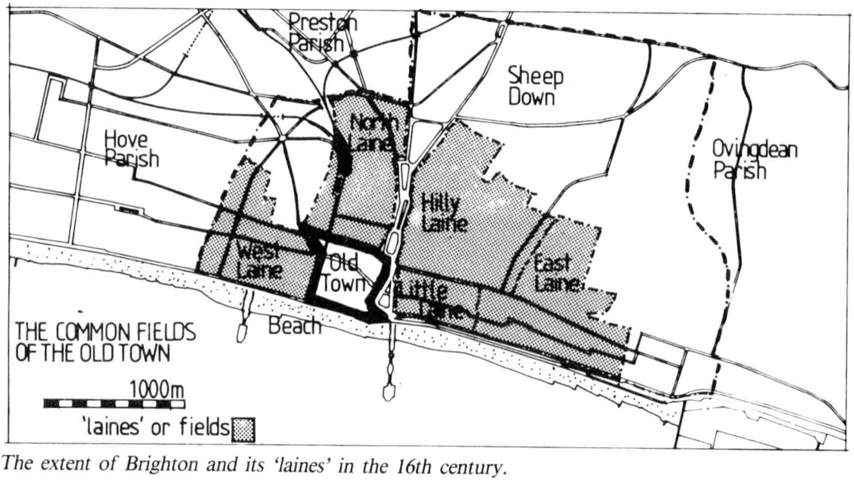

The extent of Brighton and its 'laines' in the 16th century.

system was never enclosed. When Brighton spread outside of the old town boundaries, land was sold in strips to developers and the layout of the field system came to be imprinted on the street pattern of modern Brighton. The old trackways through the fields became the main streets such as Edward Street and St. James's Street and houses were built along the strips.

During the 16th century the town's population increased as long distance fishing for cod and herring in the North Sea became more important. This was a period of rapid population growth when the countryside was unable to absorb the available labour and there was considerable migration into towns like Brighton. The town offered few restrictions to immigrants and, as the demand for accommodation increased, so the existing property owners built new cottages on vacant land within the town. In the reign of Elizabeth I Brighton's importance as a fishing town

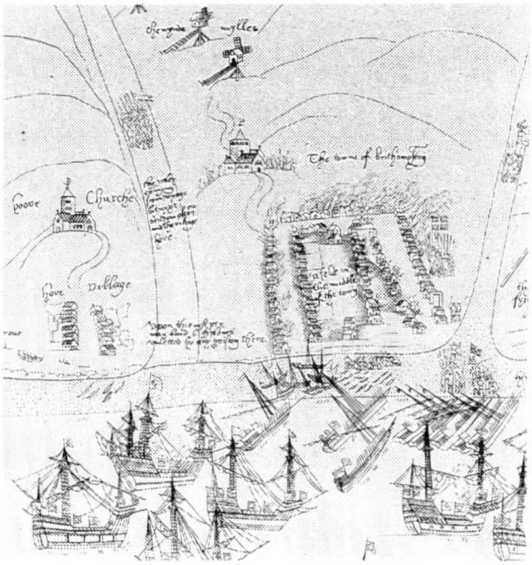

The Old Town in the 16th century.

grew considerably. Consumption of fish was increasing in Western Europe and both the Scarborough cod and Yarmouth herring industries expanded attracting fishing fleets from the coasts of Sussex and Kent. Brighton fishermen specialised mainly in herring. Fleets of boats sailed around to the east coast during the months of September and October. The fishermen were also coastal traders, sailing up to Newcastle with the profits from their fishing to buy coal which they sold along the south coast.

Between 1550 and 1640 the town's population increased from about 1,000 to 4,000, and the demand for houses led to infilling within the existing streets. During this period the grid of streets which today forms the old town became firmly established within the square contained by North Street, West Street, East Street and the cliff front. These streets enclosed an area of about 25 hectares and defined the limits of urban development until the end of the 18th century. Within this square the principal streets — Middle Street, Ship Street and Black Lion Street — all ran from south to north, containing between them substantial areas of open space.

St. Nicholas's Church.

The parish church of St. Nicholas stood alone to the north-west of the town on a low hill. During the 1640s 50 boats sailed each year to take part in the Yarmouth herring fisheries. But the industry was threatened by falling catches and the fleets from the south coast often came under attack from Dutch or French naval vessels. In addition, the beaches at Brighton were suffering from serious erosion and more and more boats were moved to new moorings in the estuary of the Adur at Shoreham. The decline of the fishing industry was rapid: during the 1680s only 30 boats remained, and the last tiny fleet of 4 boats sailed to Yarmouth in 1697. Meanwhile the town tried to develop a major role in coastal trading, but cargo boats needed small crews and the fleet was too small to absorb the local labour force, even though Brighton had, by the end of the century, the biggest cargo fleet on the south coast. Eventually the industry declined in the face of competition from the east coast. As unemployment increased the workforce drifted away from Brighton, some moving to London, some joining the Royal Navy.

By 1700 Brighton's fortunes were at a low ebb and the Justices had to apply for poor relief. Coastal erosion destroyed parts of the cliff and the market place had to be moved to a site in Black Lion Street, close to where the Ramada Hotel now stands. Attempts to build groynes to protect the cliffs failed for lack of funds.

Seaside Resort

During the early 18th century seabathing became a fashionable pastime and coastal towns like Weymouth, Hastings, Margate and Brighton were suddenly able to develop new roles as health and holiday resorts. They took over the routines and rituals of inland spas like Bath and adapted them to the seaside, adding novelties such as the newly invented bathing machine. Brighton's first recorded seabathing visitors came during the 1730s when the town was still very much cheaper than inland spas like Tunbridge Wells. Dr. Richard Russell of Lewes, a well known figure in East Sussex society, was a passionate advocate of the curative powers of spa and sea waters. After 1750 he sent patients to Brighton where he owned a house at the front of the Steine on the site now occupied by the Royal Albion Hotel. He established his own reputation and, indirectly, that of Brighton by publishing a book on the use of seawater for the treatment of various illnesses. Russell encouraged businessmen from Lewes to invest in Brighton's development as a resort, among them Samuel Shergold who became the proprietor of the new Castle Inn.

Accessibility was an important factor in Brighton's development as a resort. It was the closest south coast town to London and lay on what became after 1760 a popular route to the continent. After 1750 road transport improved considerably and the journey from London could be accomplished in about 5 hours. Proximity to Lewes and Tunbridge Wells, both centres for Sussex society, was also important during the early years when many of Brighton's visitors were drawn from the surrounding region. The number of visitors started to increase and there was considerable investment in new facilities such as lodging houses, libraries, bathing machines, and theatres. Between 1750 and 1780 most of these were established within the old town.

After 1780 Brighton's growth was spectacular and the population increased rapidly. Development now spilled out of the old town and new houses, lodging houses and service buildings appeared on farmland to the north and east of the town close to the Steine which had become a popular promenade. Most of the new development was in the form of terraces and followed the divisions of the old open field system. The old town became the business and resort centre for the new suburban residential areas.

When, George, Prince of Wales, first came to Brighton in 1783 it had already established itself as the nation's most fashionable seaside resort, and he was merely following in the footsteps of his three uncles. However, he liked the town and its proximity to London and his decision to establish his seaside home overlooking the Steine in 1784 set the seal on Brighton's popularity and inspired 4 decades of frenzied development. The Napoleonic Wars brought a threat of invasion and large numbers of troops were garrisoned around Brighton. Paradoxically the existence of such a large body of soldiers and particularly of eligible young officers added to Brighton's attractions. Jane Austen's heroine, Lydia Bennet, thought a visit to Brighton "comprised every possibility of earthly happiness", and advised her sisters: "Go to Brighton — that is the place to get husbands!"

Brighton in 1788.

This period of rapid growth also witnessed an overflowing of architectural inventiveness. Famous architects such as Holland, Porden and Nash helped to build the Prince Regent's famous marine pavilion and established a vocabulary of architectural elements which became primary constituents of Brighton's Regency style. However, it was the local trio of Charles Busby, Amon Wilds and his son Amon Henry Wilds whose joint and separate work had the most impact on Brighton, both in terms of the sheer quantity of their output and the vigour of their designs.

By 1820 the town extended from Royal Crescent in the east to Bedford Square in the west, and the population had risen in 40 years

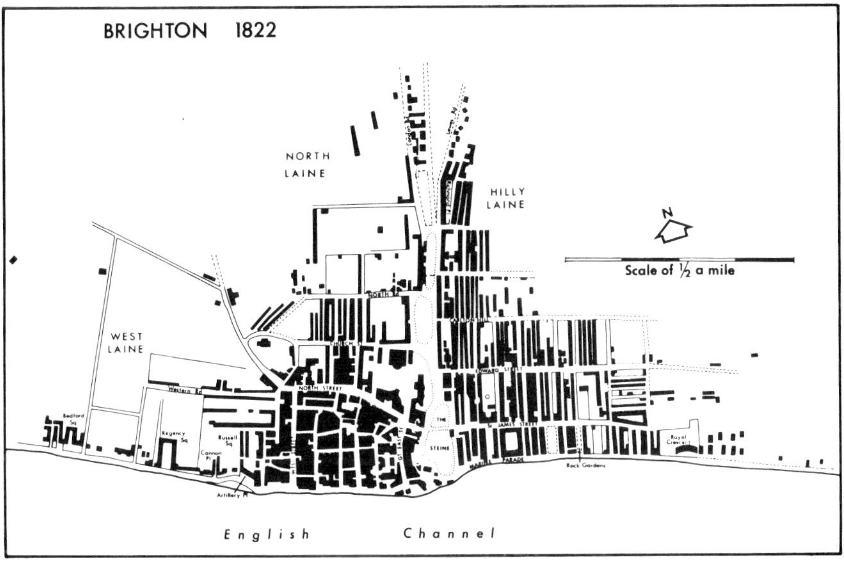

Brighton in 1822.

from 3,500 to 25,000. At that time the number of visitors in the season was about 10,000 and included people from every walk of life. Increasingly visitors would come in large family groups with their servants and expect to entertain lavishly in their own homes. The existing facilities could hardly cope with the demand, particularly for larger houses. During the 1820s enterprising developers sought to establish self-contained suburbs at Kemp Town in the east and Brunswick Town in the west. Neither development was wholly successful as a speculative venture, but both made their mark on Brighton's seafront. New churches and assembly rooms were established in these new communities and created competition with the facilities in the old town. The older housing near the centre became less popular and less expensive and much of it was converted to boarding houses and single room lodgings.

During the 1830s the rate of growth fell sharply. This was due in part to increased competition from other resorts, and in part to a general economic recession. The town faced problems of unemployment, bankruptcy, and poor return on housing investment. Concern for the future stimulated interest in a proposal for a rail link with London, and, after much debate, a line was opened in 1841. The coming of the railway coincided with an economic revival, and heralded a new period of prosperity and growth in the town. After 1841 Brighton became popular as a resort for short holidays from London. It attracted wealthy long-term visitors during the winter months and day trippers in the summer. More and more people chose to work in London and commute daily back and forth while middle class families retired to Brighton and sought modern houses in the new suburbs. Following 1840 large numbers of medium sized terrace houses were built as well as larger detached villas and during the decade the town's population rose from 45,000 to 65,000. The

The Chain Pier in 1824.

Regency style persisted into the 1850s, though it was gradually displaced by more typically Victorian preoccupations.

After 1850 the demand for new houses was exacerbated by a shortage of suitable land for new building development. Rents rose quickly with serious consequences for a community that was largely dependent upon rented accommodation. The working class poor and the unemployed were the hardest hit, and pockets of very bad slum housing developed in older parts of the town. Brighton was hemmed in by one large private agricultural holding which belonged to William Stanford and stretched from the seafront west of Brunswick to the Ditchling Road. This was the last area of land lying close to the town which was not too steep for housing development. In 1853 the estate passed to Stanford's daughter who was still a child, and only after her marriage in 1867 was land released for development. In 1854 Brighton was incorporated as a Borough, but Brunswick Town and areas to the west successfully resisted inclusion, thus laying the foundation for the separate town of Hove. The Borough of Brighton had an area of 1,100 hectares and a population of 65,000. New resort attractions, such as the West Pier, the Aquarium, the Palace Pier, various Public Baths and the large seafront hotels, were all built in Brighton, while Hove resisted tourist development, preferring to retain its image of exclusive low density residential town. Before 1854 both towns had been managed in piecemeal fashion by commissioners and churchmen and it was not until after incorporation in 1854 that municipal improvements were put into effect. By that time a proper sewerage system was long overdue: the beaches were polluted and the uncontrolled activities of factories and abbatoirs posed a serious threat to health. The growing population required ever increasing supplies of potable water and new pumping stations were needed to supply the towns from downland aquifers.

The eventual release of Stanford land allowed development in Hove to the west of Brunswick Town during the 1870s and a grid of wide avenues and rather portentious Victorian villas and terraces grew up between the railway and the sea. Brighton, meanwhile, was growing northwards on Stanford land around Preston and soon both Preston and Patcham villages were caught up in a continuous ribbon of housing development.

The late Victorian housing developments of Brighton were architecturally less distinguished than those of the earlier decades of the century, but the town did experience an enormous spate of church building by various denominations, much of it of a very high quality. During the 25 years following the arrival of the railway in 1841 the number of Anglican churches rose from 14 to 27. Two

Aerial view of Brighton — mid 19th century.

Victoria Gardens.

Brighton vicars, Henry Michell Wagner and his son Arthur Douglas, between them commissioned and financed no less than 11 churches, employing such notable architects as Carpenter and Bodley.

The Twentieth Century

During the Edwardian period the development of the European rail network tempted many of Brighton's wealthier visitors away to the warm resorts of the French and Italian coasts and to the larger and more sophisticated European spas. Winter letting declined and many houses were converted into family hotels and guest houses catering for short-stay summer visitors. Brighton increasingly had to face the problem of seasonality as tourism contracted into the summer period.

At the turn of the century Brighton's population stood at around 120,000 but the rate of growth was falling off. After 1896 the Corporation began to buy up large areas of downland outside of the town boundaries in an effort to limit development and protect water supplies. These purchases were engineered by Sir Harry Carden, a Councillor remembered as "the father of modern Brighton". During the following 30 years almost 5,000 hectares were purchased, and the town became a major agricultural landowner.

Between the wars Brighton and Hove were transformed by piecemeal suburban house-building which created a ribbon of development around both towns. This took place largely on cheap downland which became suitable for housing only with the availability of motor buses which could cope with steep hills and long distances. Interest rates were low and one local building society formed entrepreneurial partnerships with local builders to promote house-building on a large scale. The centre of Brighton was still densely populated and plagued by notoriously bad housing and there were many townsfolk who dreamt of owning a new home in the suburbs. Commuters to London also generated demand for new housing. The Corporation added to developments at the periphery by building some of the earliest suburban council housing in the country at Moulsecoomb with the intention of re-housing families from the slums. However, high rents and transport costs combined to make Moulsecoomb an impractical alternative for those in greatest need. The development of motor transport

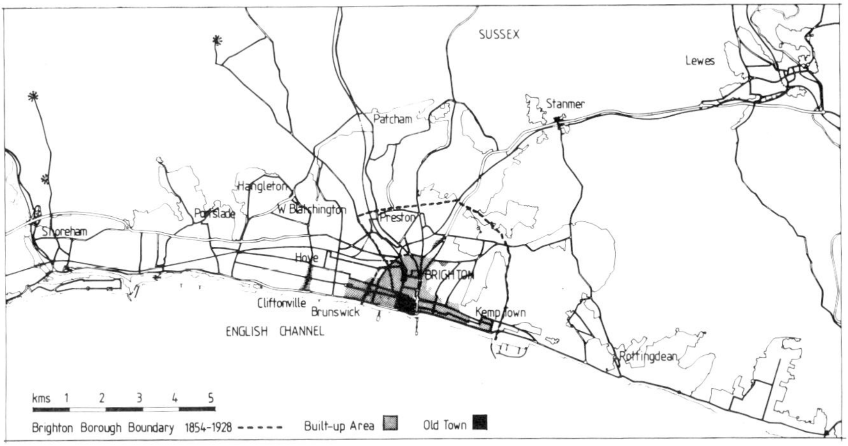

The growth of Brighton — mid 19th century.

The edge of Brighton — Coldean.

also encouraged ribbon development along the coast between Brighton and Eastbourne where the new dormitories of Peacehaven and Saltdean sprang up. In 1928 Brighton's boundaries were extended to include Rottingdean, Woodingdean and Patcham, and the town's area increased from 1,100 hectares to 5,000 hectares. Hove's boundaries were extended towards the west at about the same time.

The interwar period also saw many changes in the older parts of Brighton. In order to cater to the demands of increased traffic, many buildings were demolished to allow for street widening. New developments of shops, office buildings and banks appeared in Western Road, West Street and North Street, though these did little to enhance the spatial or architectural quality of the central area.

Brighton suffered some damage during World War II, mainly from bombs jettisoned after raids on London, and over 200 civilians were killed. After the war the town enjoyed a brief revival as a summer resort before cheap air travel lured British tourists to foreign beaches. Now its visitors are mainly trippers who come down from London for a day at the coast. Sadly it has failed to develop new facilities, or indeed to conserve existing facilities in a way likely to exploit the town's natural advantages of climate and location. The massive Marina project failed to act as a springboard for a new leisure industry and is now being replanned to accommodate a hypermarket. One pier is closed and its future is uncertain, while the other serves as an amusement arcade. Brighton's only open air swimming pool at Black Rock was recently demolished. Today the larger hotels are very much dependent on the conference trade which is attracted by the town's excellent conference facilities, by its mild climate and by its proximity to London, Gatwick Arport and the Continent.

Derelict site — The North Laine.

Typical Suburban Houses.

Although Brighton can no longer claim to be a major seaside resort its importance as a regional centre has grown, and it has succeeded in attracting considerable office development. The decision to build the new Sussex University at Stanmer in the 1960s and the subsequent development of Brighton Polytechnic have given the town a new role as an educational centre, and every summer thousands of young foreigners arrive to attend English language courses.

Attempts to redevelop parts of central Brighton have not met with much success. The much vaunted Churchill Square development offers a windswept environment to the shopper and makes a rude assault on the grain of the surrounding area. Other projected redevelopments have come to nothing and large areas of the North Laine have been condemned for decades to lie as barren wasteland. Traffic planning seems often to have put the needs of the private motorist before those of the pedestrian, and public transport is expensive and sometimes inconvenient.

After the war a large proportion of new housing was in the form of multi-storey flats, built both by the local authority and by private developers. These have rarely been sited with any regard for the scale of the surrounding area or their possible effect on the skyline. In recent years government spending cuts have curtailed local authority house building, although there has been some increase in the activities of government funded housing associations. The current failure to improve or augment the housing stock is leading to an increase in bad housing and homelessness, and the scarcity of suitable housing in every sector has made Brighton one of the most expensive towns outside of London in which to buy or rent a home.

Visitors to Brighton and Hove will look in vain for any visible dividing line between these two towns which have developed side by side and yet remain so separate, and may well wonder why they have never been forged into one larger administrative unit. Many of today's big issues such as the proposed northern by-pass call for close co-operation between the twin boroughs.

Developments during the last 40 years have done little to add to Brightons' charms while several precious things have been lost. Today there is still a lot to admire and to cherish, while there is much that should cause concern: poor facilities, congested traffic, bad housing. But Brighton remains a uniquely attractive town set in beautiful physical surroundings and possessing a priceless architectural heritage.

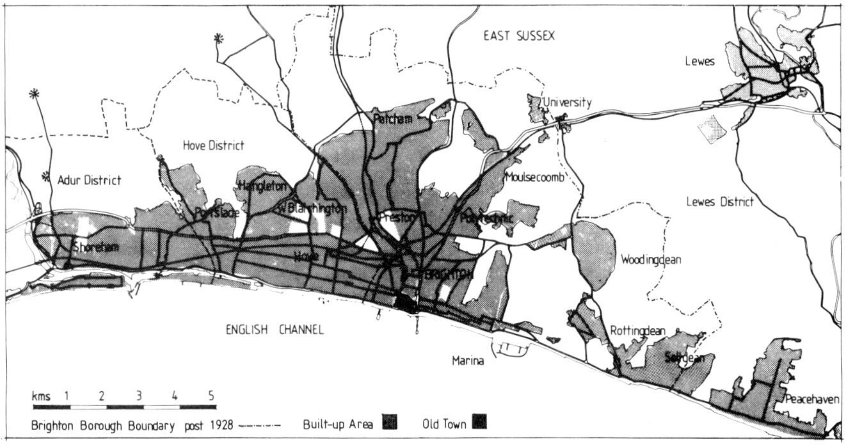

The growth of Brighton — mid 20th century.

THE WILDS & CHARLES BUSBY

The growth of Brighton as a resort town and the evolution of its Regency style can both be attributed to fashion, to demand and to the availability of capital. The subsequent manifestation of these forces in built form was largely the result of the work of three men: Amon Wilds, his son Amon Henry Wilds and his partner Charles Augustus Busby. Today hundreds of houses laid out in terraces, streets, squares and crescents and numerous public buildings bear witness to their skill and industry.

The aim here is to highlight the importance of these three architects, to evaluate their contribution to the evolution of late Georgian architecture in Brighton, and to provide a frame of reference for their various buildings and projects which are mentioned in this guide. Until quite recently their work was largely ignored and a number of their buildings have been either demolished or threatened with demolition. Sir Sacheverell Sitwell writing of Brighton in his book 'British Architects and Craftsmen' in 1945 states, without any justification: "There are the yellow stucco parades and squares of Brighton, Regency buildings, but by unknown architects, and of different treatment from the terraces of Regent's Park. There is no tendency to group the buildings into one huge classical facade". However, two years later in 1947 Antony Dale published his invaluable book Fashionable Brighton' and provided the first full and informed appraisal of the work of Busby and the Wilds. Dale pointed out that they produced between them at least as much work in Brighton as did the Woods in Bath and yet had remained relatively unknown. Recent research in architectural history has shed more light on the many sources and influences which informed the work of Busby and the Wilds, and has further squared their account with obscurity.

The astonishing success of these three provincial architects resulted partly from their ability to fulfill an unprecedented demand during the early years of the 19th century for better designed, more spacious and more elegant town houses, and partly from their skill in producing imaginative layouts for landowners and speculators which could realise the maximum commercial potential of what had hitherto been farmland. Working together and individually they were able to design in a way which revealed a keen appreciation of the Georgian classical vocabulary, a vocabulary which had been evolving for more than 70 years and which was being opened up to ever wider and more liberal interpretation.

The growing popularity and importance of Brighton between 1770 and 1820 led to a rapid increase of population. During the 18th century the number of houses in Brighton tripled from 450 to nearly 1300. After 1800 development started to spread out of the old town into the laines to the north and east. The marine pavilion which Henry Holland built for the Prince Regent after 1787 inspired the construction of other large houses in the Steine and along Marine Paradc. By 1821 the number of houses had risen to around 4,000 and Brighton extended as far as Royal Crescent to the east, as far as Richmond Place in the Steine, and westwards as far as Bedford Square.

Brighton was already well established as a resort before the Prince Regent's arrival in the 1780s, but royal patronage added to the glamour of the town. He summoned a number of highly regarded architects and artists to work on his various projects, among them Henry Holland, William Porden, James Wyatt, Humphrey Repton and John Nash. The quality and style of the work of these men was to have a lasting effect on the subsequent development of Brighton during the late Georgian and early Victorian periods.

By 1820 there was an almost insatiable demand for elegant and spacious houses on the part of wealthy residents and seasonal visitors who wished to entertain lavishly in their own homes. As the rich moved out to new developments beyond the limits of the old town there was also an added need for smaller dwellings and workshops to house the growing numbers of tradesmen, craftsmen and servants who were attracted into Brighton. This latter need was met partly by infill building within the old town and partly the development of streets of modest houses behind the grand frontage developments of the rich.

During this period the town changed in appearance and scale as well as in extent. Before 1820 houses were given shallow window bays extending upwards through only part of the facade with delicate and thin

Typical facade elements by Wilds.

decorative details. After that date the new manner which characterised the buildings of Busby and the Wilds was much more powerful and assertive. In this they were influenced by Holland's work in London, by the country houses of Robert Adam and James Wyatt, and by the strongly articulated facades of Nash in London's Regent Street and Regent's Park. Their distinctive elements were the sweeping semi-circular bay, plain, pilastered or columned, and the deep, strongly projecting cornice. They used flat fronted houses with plain facades in pairs or triplets to compose terraces, and added pilasters, columns, pediments and porticos to create palace facades out of street frontages.

The Wilds and Busby responded to four distinct kinds of development opportunity which characterised Brighton's housing boom. First there were existing houses which were required to be enlarged, extended or restyled. Second there were infill replacements for houses too small or too old to be altered and improved. Third there were new and realigned streets which offered the possibility to create ordered groups of houses as terraces, crescents and squares. Finally there were huge speculative estate developments which gave the opportunity to assemble terraces, crescents and squares alongside public and social buildings into grand town-scaled compositions in the outlying suburbs.

Charles Augustus Busby (1788-1834) was arguably the most versatile and talented of the trio. He was born in London, the son Dr. Thomas Busby, a noted musician and author. He had a natural talent for drawing and exhibited at the Royal Academy when only 13 years old. He became a pupil of D. A. Alexander and in 1807 at the age of 19 was awarded the Gold Medal of the Royal Academy School. In 1808 he published his first book, 'A Series of Designs for Villas and Country Houses'. In the preface he dismissed Robert Adam as a mannerist and imitator. In 1810 a second book illustrating designs for chimneys, folding doors, and verandas was published. These designs were later used and developed in the work of Busby and the Wilds, and the verandahs and balustraded balconies became important elements in the design of their bow-fronted houses.

In the same year Busby came to build Bristol's Commercial Coffee Rooms as the result of a competition, producing a design in the manner of the Greek revival which reaffirmed his contempt for mannerism and his preference for elegant simplicity. In 1813 he

Shell ornament in Richmond Terrace.

designed and built the Episcopal Jews Chapel in Bethnal Green with G. Maliphant and then worked for a time with L. B. Hesketh on Gwrych Castle in Denbighshire.

In 1814 Busby was declared bankrupt and he left England for America where he stayed for six years, studying amongst other things State Penitentaries and paddle-steamers. Soon after his return to England in 1820 he won second prize in a competition to design a new prison at Millbank but he lacked the means to set up a practice and went to work with Francis Goodwin who was responsible for designing a number of Commissioners' Churches. Goodwin passed on the projects for Leeds and Oldham to Busby for him to submit under his own name. Busby's Gothic designs were at first accepted by the Commissioners but later rejected by Smirke and Nash who were two of the three architects called in to advise the Surveyor General. Busby tried to enlist the support of John Soane who was the third adviser but without success. This setback made him very bitter and in 1822 he set out his grievances in a pamphlet which he sent to every Member of Parliament, every architect and every engineer in the land. Later in 1822 he abandoned London after a disagreement with Goodwin and moved to Brighton where he entered into partnership with Amon Wilds.

Amon Wilds (1762-1833) was a builder turned architect from Lewes who was working in Brighton with his son Amon Henry Wilds (1784-1857). Busby and the younger Wilds were near contemporaries and in 1822 were 34 and 38 years old respectively while Wilds senior was in his sixtieth year. Amon Wilds's business seems to have grown up in Lewes at the turn of the century. In 1806 he rebuilt the nave of All Saints' Church in Lewes in a Gothic style reminiscent of Christopher Wren, and soon after built a terrace of 4 houses in Castle Place on Lewes High Street. In 1819 two of these were converted into one house for Dr. Gideon Mantell, a palaeontologist, by Amon Henry Wilds. Here the ammonite capital, the Wilds' most famous motif, appears for the first time (see 17K). In 1815 the Wilds moved to Brighton but continued to operate in both towns as architects, builders and developers. This combination of activities was not uncommon at the time: Grainger and Stephenson in Newcastle, Wood the elder in Bath, Burton, Holland and Cubitt in London were all architect-builders in their day.

After 1815 the Wilds' practice expanded and they began to be involved with each of the four categories of residential development previously referred to, as well as with churches and public buildings. Their first important commissions came from Thomas Read Kemp, who was also from Lewes. Kemp was a wealthy landowner and was MP for Lewes until 1816 when he was forced to give up his seat by the fact of his involvement with a dissenting sect. In 1817 he commissioned the Wilds to build a chapel for his sect in Ship Street, Brighton. The chapel had a Greek temple front with Doric tetrastyle portico and a pylon shaped tower. It was later bought by the Church of England, renamed as Holy Trinity and subjected to almost total rebuilding. In the same year the Wilds built Western Lodge for Kemp's sister near what is now Sillwood Road but this was demolished at the end of the last century. In 1819 Kemp commissioned them to build the Temple, a large private house on what is now Montpelier Road. It was a square building with a central dome above its main hall, and strange splayed Egyptian columns on its main elevations. The house survives as the Brighton and Hove High School though it has been much altered. In 1820 Amon Henry designed the Unitarian Chapel in New Road (see 1F) and in 1825 Amon was responsible for the Congregational Chapel in Union Street (see 2L). During the same period they were involved with building a number of houses in the Steine and on Marine Parade, and acted as their own developers in Richmond Terrace.

It is not known why Busby came to Brighton in 1822 or why he joined forces with the Wilds. Certainly his career had failed to live up to the promise of his youth and he had made himself less than popular in the capital. Perhaps he was recruited by Kemp who was by now planning his Kemp Town development and who may have sensed the limitations of the aging Amon Wilds. The nature of the relationship between the three men has never been unravelled. All three continued to work individually. Amon Henry still teamed up with his father, but after 1822

Adam style capitals Newburgh Assembly Rooms.

Wilds in Montpelier Road.

he worked more and more by himself. Amon Wilds carried out a number of commissions in partnership with Busby, but Busby in particular was prolific as an individual. Amon Wilds died in 1833 and Busby in 1834 so that the rich period of their association lasted only 11 years. Amon Henry lived on until 1857 and continued to build in the Regency style well into the Victorian age.

The three men were continually engaged in the first category of development, refronting existing houses with elegant balustrading, balconies and bows. It is now difficult to distinguish much of their work from that of their emulators and contemporaries, or to identify their separate individual contributions. A comparison of an unchanged house such as No. 3, Old Steine with the Busby-Wilds fronts of Nos. 23 and 26 reveals the nature of their work (see 3A).

The second category of residential development involving the complete replacement of older properties can be seen in the Old Steine, Grand Parade and Marine Parade (see 3A, 3D, 7, 7A).

The third category which involved the design of composed groups of houses on new and re-aligned roads can be seen in four pre-Busby schemes carried out between 1818 and 1822 by the Wilds: Regency Square on Kings Road (see 9K), Waterloo Place, Richmond Terrace (see 3G) and Hanover Crescent (see 3H).

Regency Square was designed by the Wilds as a series of terraced houses, bow-fronted up to their first floors with a centralised composition to each face of the square. Richmond Terrace was built by Amon Henry as a speculative development over a number of years with the different groups of houses responding to the demands of the moment. The southern run of three houses is a magnificent composition of bow front, stuccoed rustication and yellow brick and offers an elegant testimony to the Wilds' skill and inventiveness during the period before they were joined by Busby.

Hanover Crescent was initiated by a local entrepreneur called Henry Brooker. Here Amon Henry Wilds introduced the notion of the crescent as a string of connected Palladian villas. Each villa element contains three houses, except for the central one which contains only two. Each is composed as a separate entity with its own central pediment and giant order of pilasters. The effect is like a succession of linked country houses. This was a theme to which he was to return periodically as, for instance, at Park Crescent (see 3K), Montpelier Crescent (see 11e) and Park Crescent in Worthing.

The first major commission which Amon Wilds and Busby tackled together was the massive Kemp Town scheme to the east of

Busby in Brunswick Square.

Wilds and Busby, the first great concept.

Brighton, an example of the fourth category of development. Kemp was the initiator and developer of the project, Wilds and Busby were his planners and architects. The original scheme was conceived in 1823 as a grand classical palace facing the seafront against a backdrop of the open downs with a network of service streets and squares tucked in behind the main sweeping facade (see 7N, 7P, 7Q). The facades were heavily rusticated up to the first floor with carefully contrived arrangements of plain wall and groups of pilasters or columns on the main floors under a pronounced cornice and attic.

A second major development was inititated in 1824 to the west of Brighton just beyond the parish boundary with Hove and was given the name 'Brunswick Town'. The inspiration came from the Kemp Town development though it is not known who was its originator. The landowner was the Rev. Thomas Scutt but he did not participate directly in the development, being content to sell blocks of land to individual builders. Amon Wilds and Charles Busby were again the architects, although it is generally believed that the work was handled by Busby alone. The development again took the form of a vast Renaissance palace with a varying pattern of columned and pilastered bays, sometimes centrally composed, sometimes forming rythmic ensembles. Busby reveals himself again to be a purist, and is strongly influenced by John Nash in his clear articulation of base, piano nobile and attic and in the depth of his facade treatment. Kemp Town and Brunswick both encountered many difficulties and were finally compromised by financial realities and by the vagaries of individual builder-developers. However, they represent the pinnacle of Busby's and Wilds' work, and must be regarded as considerable achievements in the fields of domestic architecture and town design.

Both architects continued to be involved with individual buildings. Busby designed St. George's Church in 1824 to serve the growing Kemp Town community (see 8C) and Portland Place in the following year (see 7F). Wilds built the Gothic House in Western Road in 1825 (see 10K). Little is known of their joint activities after 1827 and it is assumed that Wilds withdrew into retirement while Busby was heavily occupied with the supervision of work in Brunswick Town and Kemp Town. Amon Wilds died in 1833 and is buried in the south eastern corner of St. Nicholas's Churchyard. His imposing tombstone was designed by his son Amon Henry and describes him as a "man of considerable genius who rescued Brighton from antiquated simplicity and rusticity and restored the order of the ancient architecture of buildings". Busby died in the following year and is buried in St. Andrew's Churchyard in Hove.

Amon Wilds' tombstone.

Amon Henry Wilds lived on for another 24 years and continued to practice as an architect. His major buildings include the Royal Newborough Assembly Rooms of 1825 (see 10D), Montpelier Crescent of 1845 (see 11E) and Park Crescent from 1849 onwards (see 3K). He also worked outside of Brighton, designing Park Crescent in Worthing and Chestham Park near Henfield, both in 1830, and Gravesend Town Hall in 1836. Wilds was an eclectic and his work showed a remarkable range of architectural vocabulary. He designed Neo-Grec churches, Assembly Rooms in the manner of Robert Adam, Palladian crescents, and villas in the picturesque Italianate style.

The achievement of Amon Wilds and Charles Busby was remarkable by any standards. Working together and separately during a crucial period of 11 years they translated the architectural idiom of their day into a language which was perfectly suited to the demands of developers and public alike, and they helped to transform Brighton into a thriving Georgian resort richly endowed with magnificent streets, squares and crescents. Nor should the considerable output of Amon Henry Wilds be undervalued: he worked on alone after the deaths of his two associates and continued to produce powerful and attractive Regency buildings well into the Victorian period. Indeed it could be said that these three men played a significant part in the final stages of the last great period of architectural concensus in this country.

Amon Henry Wilds later work in Montpelier Villas.

THE WAGNERS

The church-builders and clerics Henry Michell Wagner and Arthur Douglas Wagner were to have almost as big an impact on Victorian Brighton as the Wilds and their partner Charles Busby had had on the Brighton of the late Georgian period. Henry Michell Wagner was Vicar of Brighton from 1824 to 1870 and saw the number of churches in his parish grow from three to nineteen. His son Arthur Douglas was first Curate and then Vicar of St. Paul's in West Street from 1849 to 1902. During this period he built five new churches in the town, financing them largely from his own pocket.

The growth of the town's population during the lifetime of George IV was not matched by any commensurate increase in the number of churches. Regency Brighton was the expression of a carefree and worldly society, indifferent to the church and its traditions. Its church buildings were typically light, airy and classical in spirit. But the accession of Queen Victoria in 1837 heralded an age of piety which provoked a spate of church building and led to a shift from the Classical to the Gothic style.

During the early part of the 19th century the 'dissenting' churches were making so much headway that the Government felt it necessary to give support to the established church and initiated a programme of new church building with the passing of the "Million Pound Act" and the setting up of the Commissioners for New Churches. Another reaction to the popularity of non-conformism was the call for a spiritual re-awakening and a return to the tenets of the original catholic church, and this led during the 1830s to the founding of the Tractarian Movement, or the Oxfod Movement as it came to be known. This was parallelled by a growing interest in Gothic architecture and in the mediaeval church and its liturgy. Augustus Welby Pugin (1812-1852), a meticulous student of mediaeval architecture, attempted to construct a theory of contemporary architecture which would relate 'the true principles of building with the true principles of living'. John Ruskin (1819-1900), the most influential architectural writer and scholar of his day, developed Pugin's ideas and produced a study of the architecture of Venice which was to have an enormous influence on Victorian church building.

Henry Michell Wagner (1792-1870) was made the vicar of Brighton in 1824. He was the son of Melchior Henry Wagner, a hatter to George III. After a successful academic career he had been employed as tutor to the children of the Duke of Wellington. His grandfather, Henry Michell, had been vicar of Brighton from 1744 to 1789, and his wife was the daughter of William Douglas, the Canon of Westminster.

The Parish Church of St. Nicholas before Carpenter's "improvement".

At the time of Wagner's preferment the old Parish Church of St. Nicholas (see 11B) was the main Anglican church of Brighton and was supported by two relatively new 'Chapels of Ease', the Chapel Royal in North Street (see 5R) and the chapel of St. James. The Parish Church was 'galleried to the roof' and crammed with box pews which accommodated a congregation of 1300, but the combined seating capacities of the three buildings could not have been more than about 2,500. A large proportion of the seating was rented, and relatively few 'free' pews were available for poorer parishioners, a fact which must have added to the popularity of the dissenting chapels which offered free admission. In 1824 the buildings of the established church were outnumbered by those of other denominations. There was the Union Chapel in Union Street (see 2L), Kemp's newly built Trinity Chapel in Ship Street (see 8C), the Unitarian Chapel in New Road (see 1F), Lady Huntingdon's Chapel in North Street, and the Friends' Meeting House (see 2K) as well as a Roman Catholic chapel and a Jewish synagogue. Interestingly the first three of these were the work of the Wilds Partnership and were all built in a classical style.

It was quite common for Anglican churches to be put up by speculative builders, sold to a preacher or his financial backers and then run as a business concern, the pews being disposed of by auction to the highest bidder. Such churches did not always win immediate recognition from the established church and often ran for years as dissenting chapels. This was the case with St. James' Chapel which had been finished in 1810 but was not consecrated until 1817 when it was 'bought' by Nathanial Kemp from the original consortium which had built it.

Between 1824 and 1830 five new Anglican Churches were created in Brighton. This burst of activity was partly due to the support given by the Commissioners for New Churches, partly to the encouragement of the new vicar, and partly to the activities of developers keen to profit from a situation of short supply. St. Margaret's near Regency Square, a proprietory chapel built in 1824 by the entrepreneur Barnard Gregory, was designed in the Neo-Grec style with a full tetrastyle Ionic portico. It was finally demolished in 1959. St. George's Church in Kemp Town was designed in 1824 in a typical Georgian Classical style by Charles Busby for Thomas Read Kemp (see 8C). St. Mary's Chapel in Rock Gardens was built in 1827 to designs by Amon Henry Wilds based on the Temple of Nemesis in Athens. It was demolished during the 1870s to make way for Emerson's St. Mary the Virgin (see 8F). Kemp's Trinity Chapel in Ship Street was bought by the Church of England in 1825, converted for orthodox use and renamed as Holy Trinity Church. Much later in the century it was completely 'Gothicised' by Somers Clarke.

St. Mary's Chapel: "unconverted heathenism".

St. Peter's in 1839.

The most important of the five new additions, however, was St. Peter's on the Level (see 3L). This was the first church building project with which Henry Michell Wagner was directly involved. In the competition which was held to select the architect a Gothic design by Charles Barry was chosen in preference to a Classical design from the Wilds-Busby Partnership. Barry was essentially a Georgian architect. His design is light and fanciful and totally lacks the archaeological authenticity which was to categorise the true Gothic Revival, a fact which was later underlined by Somers-Clarke's more orthodox extension. However it marked a turning point in the evolution of Brighton's church architecture.

St. Peter's East Door by Somers Clarke.

Wagner was a Georgian Vicar and a High Churchman of the Old School. But he was also an ardent and dedicated clergyman who devoted much of his considerable personal wealth to the improvement of his parish. During his lifetime the population of Brighton grew considerably and with it the power of his position. His parish was once described wistfully by the Bishop of Chichester as 'a bishopric within a bishopric'. From the moment of his preferment he showed deep concern for the poor of his parish and campaigned for the greater provision of free pews. This became one of the issues in the controversies which surrounded the building of St. Peter's. At the time of its completion in 1828 1,100 of the 1,800 pews were set aside as free places. By 1830 it was estimated that there were 18,000 'poor people' living in Brighton but only 3,000 free pews existed to accommodate them in the Anglican churches.

The first church to be initiated by Wagner was All Souls' in Eastern Road. It was built in 1833 to a classical design by Mew, who had also designed the Wagners' new Jacobean vicarage in Montpelier Road. It was the first Anglican Church to open its doors to the poor, but, according to Goodhart-Rendel, this invitation was backed up by "no architectural attractions". It cost £3,000 to build: Wagner supplied £150 of this from his own pocket while the rest came from the parish and from various private donations. The church was later gothicised by Edmund Scott, and was finally demolished in 1968.

In 1838 Wagner built Christ Church in Montpelier Road. This was designed by John Cheesman in a 'snug' 13th century Gothic style with a spire said to have been modelled on that of Chichester Cathedral. Two thirds of the 1,000 pews were free. The building was demolished in 1982 to make way for a housing scheme (see 10L). Cheesman also designed St. John's on Carlton Hill in 1840 for Wagner, reverting to a Doric classicism which Goodhart-Rendel dismisses as "ignorant beyond belief". It is now used as a Greek Orthodox church (see 8Q).

In 1845 Wagner commissioned R. C. Carpenter, after Butterfield the greatest of the Tractarian architects, to design St. Paul's Church in West Street. An imposing structure of flint with white limestone dressings, capped by a fine timber spire, this is arguably one of Brighton's most impressive Victorian churches, and perhaps Wagner's outstanding achievement (see 5J). Although it was commissioned only 5 years after St. John's it seems to belong to a different age. Wagner had never joined the Tractarian Movement but, towards the end of his life, he fell increasingly under its influence. He built St. Paul's specifically for his son Arthur Douglas Wagner who was about to be ordained, and who was later to become a leading Tractarian and ritualist. The church opened in 1848 and Arthur Douglas became its vicar one year later. St. Paul's incorporated such devices as the rood screen and the stalled chancel, signalling the emergence of a new and more elaborate form of ritual and thus sparking of a controversy which was to continue in Brighton for another half century. For many the new rituals brought the church too close to Roman Catholicism and the morning service was described in a pamphlet as: "Sunday Opera at St. Paul's".

The building of St. Paul's also marked the final triumph of the Gothic over the Classical style. Classical architecture had come to be regarded as dishonest in its suppression of different functional elements behind a generalised facade; it was foreign and it was pagan. After 1850 no new Classical churches were built in Brighton, and many of the existing ones were savagely 'gothicised'. Indeed architectural controversy seems at times to have equalled doctrinal controversy in the heat it generated. John Sawyer in his book 'The Churches of Brighton' written in 1880 dismisses the churches of the Regency, describing St. Mary's Chapel by Amon Henry Wilds as: "one of the worse built public edifices ever erected." (sic). Goodhart-Rendel, writing in 1918 in the Architectural Review, complains of the "spiritual apathy reflected in the church buildings of the early 19th century". He applauds Somers Clarke's transformation of Holy Trinity Church in Ship Street while referring to the last vestiges of Wilds's original work as "unconverted heathenism", and dismisses St. George's as "an ugly building of the usual galleried kind, with an Ionic frontispiece crowned by an irrelevant Doric cupola".

St. George's: "an ugly building of the usual galleried kind".

On Sunday, March 30th in 1851 a census of church attendance was held in Brighton. At the time there were 38 places of worship with a total 24,000 available pews: sufficient to seat one third of the town's population. Of these 12 were of the Church of England and together accommodated 13,500 worshippers. The census showed that a total of 36,000 people, half of the town's population, attended church at sometime during the day. The results of the census were used to justify further rounds of church building!

Wagner passed two further commissions to R. C. Carpenter. The first, in 1847, was for the Church of All Saints in Compton Avenue which was built to serve the new western suburbs of Brighton. It was built in a Gothic style similar to that of St. Paul's and used flint in its construction. It was finally demolished in 1957. The second, in 1853, was for the remodelling of the Parish Church of St. Nicholas. Carpenter was apparently more impressed by his own version of the Gothic than by the real thing. for he all but dismantled the old building.

Wagner's last project was the building of St. Anne's in Burlington Street which was designed in 1862 by Benjamin Ferrey, a pupil of Pugin. At this time Brighton was still one vast parish. However, it now contained 19 Anglican Chruches of which 16 had been opened by Wagner, 8 had been personally initiated by him, and a further 2 had been built by his son, Arthur Douglas.

Henry Michell Wagner preached his last sermon in September 1870 and died on October 7th in the same year. He had ruled his enormous parish for 46 years, spending much of that time embroiled in one controversy or another, and he had made many enemies. After his death his youngest son wrote of him: "If he had been less masterful his work would have been less masterly". His death marked the end of an era: his successor, the Rev. John Hannah, presided over the dismantling of the parish, and the Chapels of Ease were given districts or parishes of their own.

Arthur Douglas Wagner (1824-1902) was the eldest of Henry Michell's three sons and the only child of his first marriage. He was educated at Eton and Cambridge, and was ordained into the Church of England in 1849. In the same year he became perpetual curate to the Church of St. Pauls which had been built for him by his father. At the time of his ordination the church was a bare shell with plain glass in its windows. Arthur Douglas Wagner was a committed member of the Tractarian Movement and he set about completing the interior of the church to suit its prescribed rituals, employing such artists as Kempe and Pugin for the stained glass and Carpenter and Bodley for the interiors. In 1873, with the dismantling of the Parish of Brighton, Wagner was made vicar of St. Paul's and immediately abolished the last of the private pews.

St. Martin's: the Altar and Reredos by Somers Clarke.

Like his father, Arthur Douglas was a great church builder. He also used his wealth to finance smallscale housing developments which provided homes for his poorer parishioners and is estimated to have built over 400 houses during his lifetime. His Tractarian views involved him in continuous controversy. The rituals which he introduced at St. Pauls aroused deep opposition, as did his support for the unfortunate Rev. John Purchase who was brought to trial before an ecclesiastical court and charged with 33 separate illegal liturgical pracrtices. Wagner was also implicated in the famous trial of Constance Kent, a girl who had murdered her half-brother and came to him with her confession. At the trial Wagner refused to divulge the details of what the girl had told him and thus involved himself publicly in the controversy surrounding the status of the confessional in the Church of England.

The Tractarians of Oxford stood for doctrinal reform within the Church of England, while in Cambridge the Ecclesiologists were interested in the reform of liturgy and church building. Arthur Douglas Wagner was involved with both groups and probably influenced his father in the choice of R. C.

Carpenter, an architect supported by the Ecclesiological Society, to design St. Paul's. The Ecclesiologists favoured designs which differentiated the chancel from the nave, separating them by a chancel arch. The various parts of a church, the chancel, nave, porch, vestry and tower, were all to be clearly expressed in a free asymmetrical composition. The Gothic of the 'Decorated' or 'Middle Pointed' Period was favoured as being simple and economical. Decoration was to be concentrated around the altar, and the nave was to be lofty and plain. The Ecclesiologists argued for the construction of special 'town churches', in the poorer urban districts, buildings of imposing height with clear unobstructed interiors which would accommodate large congregations. Wagner was very much influenced by all of these ideas and sought to employ like-minded architects.

In 1862 he built the Church of St. Mary and St. Mary Magdalene in Bread Street using G. F. Bodley as his architect. The church was situated in the heart of a poor district and Wagner paid for the construction out of his own pocket. The design used plain white walls and a simple timber roof. In 1950 the building was demolished along with much of the surrounding part of the North Laine to make way for a commercial development which never materialised. In 1864 he completed the

Figure of the Virgin, the Annunciation.

Church of the Annunciation in Washington Street, another modest church built out of his own pocket in a poor district of the town. It was designed by a local surveyor called William Dancy and was later enlarged by Edmund Street.

Arthur Douglas Wagner's most important project was the building of St. Bartholomew's Church in 1872 (see 4G). For this his architect was Edmund Street. The church has the tallest nave of any in the country and was built

The Annunciation, Washington Street.

St. Martin's, Lewes Road.

almost entirely of brick at a total cost of £18,000. The building encountered violent opposition, and plunged Wagner into another storm of controversy. Critics at the time described the building as "Noah's Ark" and "Wagner's Folly", though for Goodhart-Rendel "the severe beauty of its design and its great size combine to produce an effect, unrivalled of its kind, which is impossible to describe".

In the same year Wagner commissioned Somers Clarke to build St. Martin's in Lewes Road (see 12A), in memory of his father. This was Somers Clarke's first major commission, and is built of brick in a 13th century Gothic style. Here is a town church which embodies many of the principles of the Ecclesiologists. Today it is one of the largest churches in Brighton and its situation on busy Lewes Road belies a magnificent interior.

The last of the great series of Wagner churches was the Church of the Transfiguration in Russell Street which was designed by R. H. Carpenter in 1878. The owner of an adjoining brewery protested his rights to light and Carpenter was forced to bury the church 5 metres below pavement level in order to achieve the height which Wagner required. It failed to attract congregations and suffered from problems of damp. In 1912 it was converted for use as a meat store and was finally demolished in 1966.

Arthur Douglas Wagner died in 1903 following several years of creeping infirmity. He was a mild man when compared to his father but his uncompromising adherence to his own beliefs and principles made him a figure of equal controversy. Between them father and son had built 11 churches in Brighton, providing much of the finance from their own pockets, and had exerted an enormous influence on the life of the town.

1 THE PAVILION ESTATE

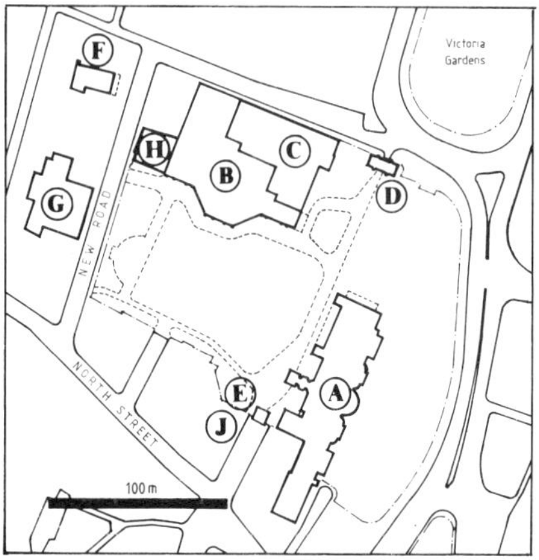

The Pavilion Gardens lie between the old town and the new, and close by the Steine, the meeting point of all the main roads into Brighton and the hub of the town's bus network. Here is the symbolic, the physical and the cultural centre of Brighton, and the ideal starting point for a tour of its buildings.

1A The Royal Pavilion

In 1785 George, Prince of Wales, entered into a clandestine marriage with Maria Fitzherbert, an Irish widow. He installed Mrs. Fitzherbert in Brighton and, in the following year, leased 'Brighton House' a farmhouse overlooking the Steine, so as to be near to his secret bride. Thus began the 35 year long saga of building and alteration which resulted finally in the oriental fairytale palace which we know today.

The Royal Pavilion stands as the legacy of a profligate prince and has become the symbol both of the style which he unwittingly promoted and the town which he made fashionable. Today it is Brighton's most prominent and best known architectural landmark. Its immediate neighbours are the Museum, the Library, the Dome Conert Hall, the Corn Exchange, the Pavilion Theatre and the Theatre Royal. Linking all of these is a small tree-lined square known as the Pavilion Gardens. These Gardens have recently been remodelled according to the original plans of John Nash, drawn perhaps 170 years ago and never executed at the time. The Gardens offer a rare opportunity to the visitor to sit and relax in the open air.

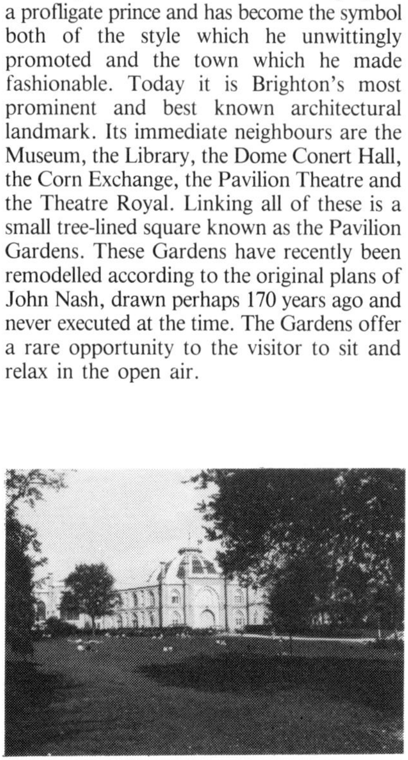

The Pavilion Gardens.

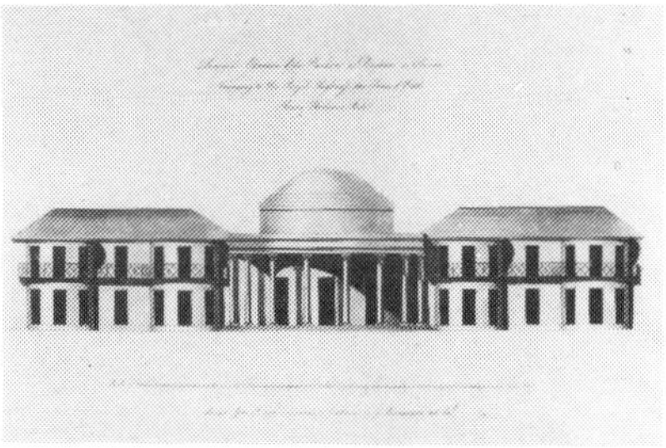

1A Holland's Marine Pavilion.

In 1787 Henry Holland, who was also the Prince's architect for Carlton House in London, was engaged to enlarge and refurbish the farmhouse to suit the grandiose needs of royalty. Holland effected the transformation of farmhouse into marine pavilion by adding a domed rotunda behind a detached Ionic colonnade with a new wing balancing the original. Today the circular plan and dome of the saloon are the only visible reminders of the original building though much of it was incorporated within the later building stages.

The Prince was without doubt a difficult client, constantly responding to new notions and swayed by change in taste and fashion. By 1801 he had grown dissatisfied with his Brighton home and Holland was recalled to make further changes. He now added a new entrance portico and hall, a conservatory and three new staircases. His collaborator on this

1A The Royal Pavilion.

1A Part section showing Music Room and Salon.

1A Interior of Banqueting Room.

1A East elevation.

occasion was the decorator Frederick Crace who was responsible for the introduction of Chinoiserie to the interiors, and whose firm was to be involved with all subsequent stages of development.

While Holland was busy with the Pavilion the Prince employed William Porden to build new stables on land to the west of the Pavilion (see 1B). Porden was inspired in part by the water colour views of India which had recently been published by Thomas and William Daniell and designed a monumental building the Indo-Saracenic Style. Once finished the stables provoked the comment that the Prince's horses were better housed than he and soon he was making plans for a new round of improvements to the Pavilion! Several architects, including Porden himself and Humphrey Repton were to submit plans over the new few years, but building was delayed by lack of funds until 1812 when James Wyatt took over. However, Wyatt died a year later and was replaced finally by John Nash.

Nash buried the bulk of Holland's work under a mantle of Hindoo, Mahometan and even Gothick decorations. Exploiting new materials and the latest construction techniques he built the huge central dome over the Saloon and the curious ten-like roofs of the Banqueting Hall and the Music Room. His use of cast iron was highly original as, for instance, in the kitchen where four slender columns which support the roof lantern terminate in palm leaf capitals. The details of the interior were entrusted to the firm of Frederick Crace and the designer Robert Jones. Jones designed the Banqueting Hall with its vivid blue saucer ceiling crowned by a cluster of plantain leaves below which hovers a fierce gilt dragon clutching in its claws a massive gasolier, and the Music Room with its vast dome of gilded scallop shells springing from an octaganol cornice with supporting dragons and serpents and its rich murals of crimson and gold. It was said at the time that no words could describe the atmosphere and excitement of these rooms; this is still true today, and they must be seen to be appreciated!

The Prince finally came to the throne as George IV in 1820, two years before building work was completed. Affairs of state prevented him from enjoying his creation to the full and he died in 1830. He was succeeded by his brother William who was a regular visitor to Brighton during the seven years of his short reign, and who commissioned several new additions including the North Gateway.

Queen Victoria was a less regular visitor, however, and in 1846 Parliament voted to sell the Pavilion in order to raise money to complete Buckingham Palace. Thanks to timely action by Lewis Slight, Brighton's Town Clerk, the Pavilion was purchased by the town, but not before the interiors had been totally stripped of their decorations and furnishings. During the following century the buildings came to be used variously as Assembly Rooms, as an Art Gallery and even, during the First World War, as a Military Hospital. Only after the Second World War was there a revival of interest in the Pavilion and then began the long, slow process of restoration which is today almost complete. Once again the visitor may enjoy the Pavilion more or less as it was in its heyday.

1A Detail of east elevation.

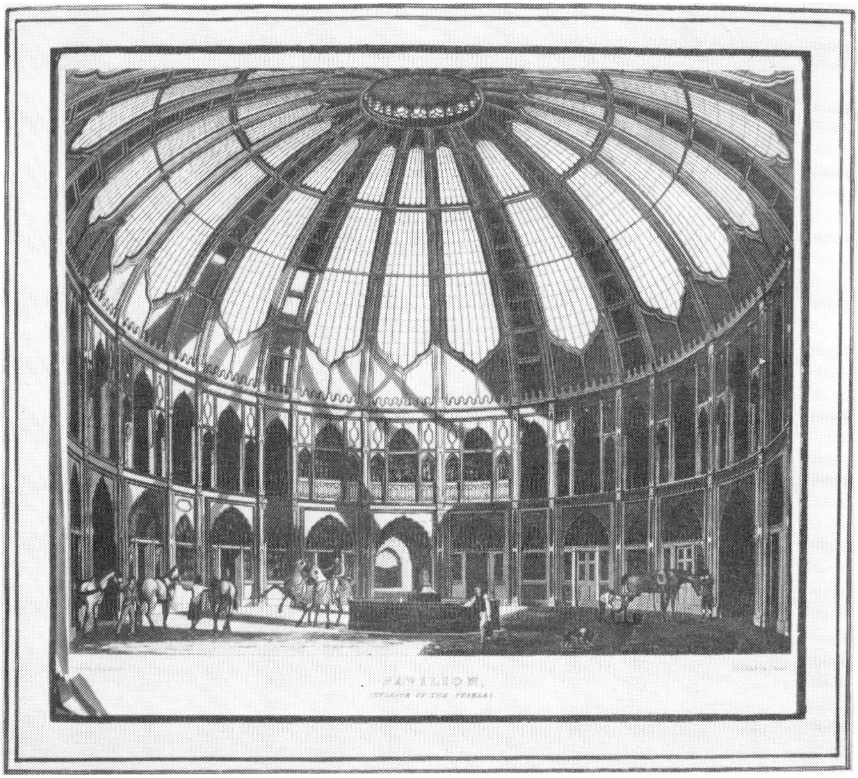

1B The Dome and the Corn Exchange Church Street

The Stables which were originally incorporated into Holland's scheme soon proved to be inadequate and in 1803 the Prince of Wales commissioned William Porden to design a new Riding House. Porden, a pupil of Samuel Pepys Cockerell, modelled the stables on the Corn Market in Paris, covering the main hall with a vast dome, 24 metres in diameter, and 19 metres high. Stabling for 44 horses was incorporated around the dome's perimeter, with space for carriages and harnesses provided in an adjoining courtyard. The dome itself consisted of glass segments separated by stuccoed ribs with a large ventilator at its crown. The construction was quite daring in its day and there were many who predicted that it would collapse when the scaffolding was removed. Progress was held up at various times when the Prince was unable to pay his bills, and it was said that Edward Saunders, one of the principal contractors, was killed by the worry of it all.

The external elevations were treated in a Mahometan-Indian style, rendered in brick with stone decorations.

The buildings were acquired by the town in 1850 and were converted for use as Assembly Rooms in 1867. During the 1930s the Dome was converted by Robert Atkinson into a modern concert hall, and the western Riding Hall became the exhibition space which is known today as the Corn Exchange. The present entrance and cloakrooms on Church Street were added in a facsimile style at a later date.

1B The Dome.

1D The North Gateway.

1C The Museum and Library
Church Street

Porden's original scheme included a building to house the Royal Tennis Courts to the immediate east of the Stables, but the Royal Purse was empty and it was never built. The site remained undeveloped until Queen Adelaide commissioned the architect Joseph Good to build additional stables during the 1830s. These stables were later converted in 1871 by the Borough Surveyor into a Town Museum. In 1889 further changes were made to create a lending library commemorating Queen Victoria's Jubilee. In 1901 a new southern entrance to the Dome was built in order to reduce congestion in Church Street.

1C The Museum and Library.

1D The North Gateway
Victoria Gardens

King William IV built the North Gateway in 1832. Good was the supervising architect, but it may be that Nash supplied the drawings. It forms a grand entrance of Bath and Portland stone capped by an oriental copper dome and is quite appropriate to the spirit of the Pavilion. To the east of the Gateway is a statue of George IV. This is a bronze copy of the original by Sir Francis Chantrey which stands in Windsor Castle.

1E The South Gateway
North Street

The original lodge at the southern entrance to the Pavilion Gardens was demolished in 1851 along with much of the original south wing of the Pavilion as part of a scheme to widen North Street. New gates were erected in their place by the Brighton Town Commissioners soon after they acquired the Pavilion Estate. During the First World War the Pavilion was used as a hospital for wounded Indian troops, apparently following

1E The South Gateway.

a suggestion from the King Emperor George V. Those who died were cremated at a special burning ghat on the South Downs where a simple white kiosk memorial stands to this day (see 13G). After the war the 'princes and peoples' of India subscribed to a memorial gateway to replace the gates of 1860. The new gateway was designed by Thomas Tyrwhitt and opened in 1921 by the Maharaja of Patiala. Built in a sombre Gujerati style it is perhaps the only part of the Pavilion to aspire to any degree of stylistic authenticity.

1F The Unitarian Chapel (Christ Church)
New Road

Originally the main road northwards from the old town followed the line of East Street and crossed along the western front of the Pavilion. The Prince was less than happy to see the world passing by his doorstep and became doubly irritated when the ever increasing traffic came between him and his newly constructed stables. In 1806 he employed Porden, his architect for the stables, to construct the New Road as a diversion to the west of his property and closed off his section of East Street to the public. In order to finance this operation he was obliged to sell off his remaining land-holding to the west of the line of the proposed road. One plot was bought by John Chatfield who later commissioned Amon Henry Wilds to build the present Unitarian Chapel in 1820. The church has an imposing stuccoed Greek tetrastyle portico which rises a little abruptly from the pavement. It was refurbished in 1966 by K. Taylor, ARIBA.

1G The Theatre Royal
New Road

Brighton's popularity as a resort arose during the second half of the 18th Century, and new demands were placed upon the cultural resources of the town. In 1764 the first theatre opened in a barn on the west side of the Steine. In 1774 a second theatre opened in North Street in purpose-built premises put up by a local bricklayer called Samuel Payne. This venture ran on for 15 years until it finally closed and the building was converted to a printing office. In 1788 a rival theatre had opened in Duke Street and it adopted the name 'Theatre Royal' after a visit by the Prince of Wales in 1805. In 1807 the Theatre Royal moved to its present premises on the west side of the recently constructed New Road facing across the Pavilion Gardens towards the entrance of the Royal Pavilion.

1G The Theatre Royal, Duke Street.

IF The Unitarian Chapel

The site was one of a number of plots sold by the Prince to finance the road and the original conveyance carries his signature. The name of the architect is not known and little remains of the original building apart from the staircase at the rear of the stalls. The stuccoed facade was on three storeys and was fronted by a Doric colonnade which sheltered the five entrance doors and inspired similar colonnading along the whole of the west side of the street. Today only the colonnades fronting Nos 6 and 7 are original.

In 1866 Henry Nye Chart bought the theatre and embarked upon extensive alterations. His architect was Charles Phipps who was a renowned theatre designer and had already built 'Theatre Royals' in both Bath and Nottingham. Phipps raised the building to incorporate a third gallery above the existing two and added a conservatory bar above the colonnade. The three galleries were horse-shoe shaped and supported on slender cast-iron columns. The structure of the auditorium remains today much as it was in 1866 though the decor has been much altered in successive refurbishments. In 1894 new and stringent fire regulations provoked a new round of alterations. Clayton and Black, a local firm of architects, incorporated No 9 New Road to create a new foyer and box office, and Phipps' conservatory was extended upwards to provide extra accommodation on each level. The original stucco facade was now clothed in red brick with stone dressings and flanked by octagonal turrets with copper domes. The colonnade was replaced with the present paired Corinthian columns and the building was extended through the block to Bond Street to create a new stage door. A final refurbishment of the interior was carried out in 1927 by the architects Sprague and Barton and resulted in the theatre which we see today.

1G The Theatre Royal.

1H The Pavilion Theatre
New Road

The Pavilion Theatre is the latest of a long series of additions and modifications to the Pavilion complex. It was designed by Robert Atkinson, and built in 1937 at the western corner of the Corn Exchange on a site formally occupied by the Dome Cottage and the stables of Mrs. Fitzherbert. It attempts to match the spirit of the Dome after a cut-price utilitarian fashion.

1J Royal Insurance Building.

1J Royal Insurance Building
Pavilion Buildings

This pleasing Neo Georgian building was designed by John Leopold Denman for the Brighton and Hove Herald and was completed in 1932. Denman was the third in a line of architects. His grandfather had been responsible for additions to St. Paul's Church (see 5J) and his father had designed Lewes Town Hall (see 17K). At the ground floor there are seven principal bays, arched in portland stone, with additional end bays containing secondary doors. Alternate arched openings contain delicate timber bay windows. The upper floors are built with handmade bricks and capped by a projecting brick cornice. The 9 bays reduced to 8 on the first and second floors with the windows centring on the ground floor piers. Joseph Cribb of Ditchling was responsible for the stone carving which includes delightful acanthus capitals decorated with tiny sea-horses and scallops. Denman and Cribb also worked together on what is now the Allied Irish Bank in the Steine where small carved panels illustrating various building craftsmen include a portrait of Denman himself as the architect. Later Denman was joined by his son, the fourth of the line, and together they designed the North Street Barclays Bank in 1956.

2 THE LANES

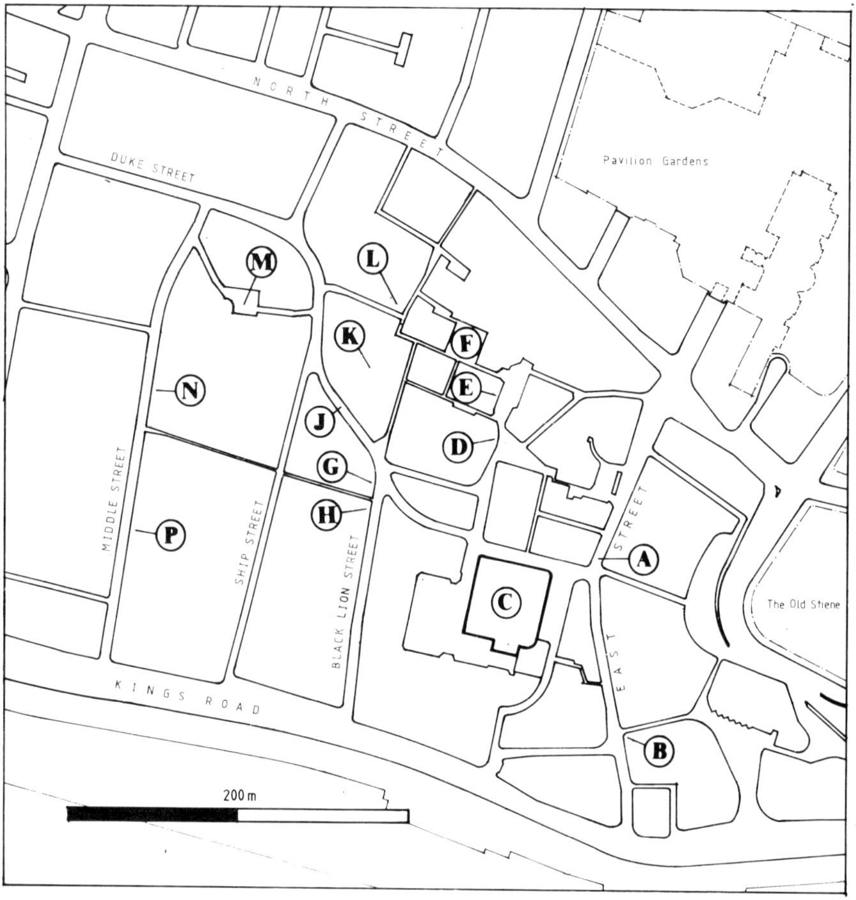

The area bounded by North, East and West Streets and the King's Road corresponds to the old town of Brighthelmston as it existed up until the mid eighteenth century. It is referred to loosely today as 'The Lanes' because of the many narrow alleyways or 'twittens' which cut across it. The principal streets, Middle Street, Ship Street, Black Lion Street and Market Street, all run from south to north though only Ship Street connects through to North Street. Of the east — west streets, Prince Albert Street was cut through in the nineteenth century, and Duke Street was created out of the widening of an earlier lane.. The lanes snake between the streets, and are often as little as a couple of metres wide. The popularity of these narrow alleyways leads one to question the validity of current planning codes which make it almost impossible to recreate this scale of urban space in modern developments.

Although Brighthelmston had a long history as a fishing town, there are no secular buildings left today which predate the 16th century. Mediaeval Brighton seems to have stood on land which was partially eaten up by the sea. The chalk cliffs of Sussex are extremely vulnerable to coastal erosion and, during the hundred years preceding 1350, almost 50 acres of town land appear to have been lost. During the 16th century the town was twice sacked by French raiders and St. Nicholas Church (11B), which stood on a hill outside of the town, was one of the few buildings to have survived through that period. In earlier times many of the town's buildings had been constructed of mud and wattle. However, during the latter part of the 16th century there was a shift to more durable materials such as flint and cobble, and clay tiles were introduced from the Low Countries. The traditional mediaeval "Hall House" form was gradually displaced by storeyed houses with brick chimneys. A few of these 17th century buildings remain to this day though they have been much altered.

In 1740 there were 450 houses in the town. Most of these were built along the north south streets, and generous areas of land remained behind them to serve as garden allotments and open ground for drying nets. Transverse pathways at this time served to give access to gardens, and to neighbouring streets.

The growing popularity of Brighton after 1750 led to the development of new land outside the old town, but much redevelopment also took place within it. New houses and workshops came to be built in the backland areas along the transverse pathways and these developed into the narrow alleyways which are now referred to as twittens. Perhaps the best example of a twitten is Black Lion Lane which runs from beside 'The Cricketers' in Black Lion Street to Ship Street and on to Middle Street. One consequence of the developments which accompanied Brighton's transformation from fishing town to fashionable resort is the fact that a large proportion of the buildings which stand today date from the end of the 18th and the beginning of the 19th centuries. During the present century there have been several proposals to redevelop the area with wider streets and modern buildings. Happily a number of the lanes have survived this threat and recent developments such as those at Brighton Square, Duke's Lane and Clarence Yard have actually attempted to recreate the scale and atmosphere of the old town.

2A East Street

East Street marked the eastern edge of the old town and was always one of its most important thoroughfares. In former times it continued northwards and formed the beginning of the route up the valley of the Wellsbourne towards Lewes, but as the Royal Pavilion developed the Prince Regent became unhappy with the amount of traffic passing by his front door and caused the street to be closed above its junction with North Street. He built New Road as a diversion one block to the west, but the traffic shifted eastwards into the Steine instead.

During the 1750s East Street had come to be regarded as the fashionable end of town: Doctor Russell, who had established his clinic close by on Pool Valley, lodged his patients in East Street, and Samuel Sharegold built his 'Castle Inn' on what later came to be called Castle Square at the junction with North Street. The Castle Inn flourished and remained one of Brighton's most popular hotels until 1822 when it as bought by George IV who converted its ballroom into his private chapel. In 1850 the southern portion of the Pavilion was demolished to allow North Street to be widened and the chapel was removed to Montpelier Place where it can still be seen (see 11G).

Today East Street contains few buildings which are really old and consists mainly of modern shops inserted into the ground floors of Victorian shells. The corner with Castle Square was recently rebuilt as a shop with offices above. Here an attempt has been made to design in a modern idiom which echoes Regency forms. Sadly the result is neither a good modern building nor a satisfactory copy and underlines the dangers inherent in the method of pastiche infilling which is currrently promoted by planners and conservationists alike.

2A East Street looking north with Brill's Baths.

2B The ABC Cinema
East Street

The site was originally occupied by Brill's Baths, one of Brighton's early bathing houses which was rebuilt in 1869 to designs by George Gilbert Scott.

The present cinema was designed by William Glen in 1929 and opened as 'The Savoy'. In its original configuration it could hold an audience of 3,000 people and accommodated 300 cars in its basement. More than a million Sussex bricks were used in the construction and the whole building is clad in glazed white terracotta tiles, a fact which earned it the name 'the white whale'. Although the building's scale is somewhat out of sympathy with its neighbours to the north, it does provide an interesting transition to the seafront. In 1976 it was converted into four mini cinemas, and its underground car park is now used as a garage.

2B The Savoy Cinema (now the ABC).

2C The Town Hall

The Town Hall was designed by local architect and sometime town councillor Thomas Cooper and was built in 1830. In its original design it took the form of a Greek cross with two storeyed porticos on each of its four arms but site problems prevented the completion of the southern arm. The completed porticos have a lower order of Doric and upper of Ionic but the relative proportions of the two

2C The Town Hall.

orders are uncomfortable. The building opened to a barrage of criticism: "Designed after a day trip to Greece", "A worse attempt at architecture was never made". All of this must have been highly embarrassing for Mr. Cooper, particularly as it was whispered that he had used his official position to secure the commission in the first place! The Town Hall was extended in 1899 and the present impressive interior staircase dates from that time. Today the building is unhappily surrounded and happily dwarfed by the Ramada Hotel development (9C), which includes a wing of new office accommodation for the Council.

2D The Pump House

Brighton Place was originally known as the Knab, a Scandinavian word meaning a small hill. There was a public pump here in the early 18th century and it was surrounded by a warren of small shops and houses. The Pump House is perhaps one of the oldest buildings in the Lanes, but much of what is visible today is of recent origin. Its facade is clad in glazed black mathematical tiles which date from the early part of the last century, and the bow windows contain modern glazing bars. A fireplace bears the date 1776, but it is also thought to have been an addition and the structure must be much older. The interiors are now disappointing.

2D The Pump House.

2E The Druid's Head
The original building on this site was probably a cottage built during the 16th century. Beer was sold here after 1830 and it received a full licence in 1856. Although it has been much altered it is one of the few houses to retain a flint front of a type which must once have been commonplace in the old town.

2E The Druid's Head.

2F Brighton Square
Brighton Square is a modern development which was built in 1966 to replace a group of derelict buildings. The architects were Fitzroy Robinson and Partners. Here an attempt has been made to create contemporary buildings in keeping with the scale of the surrounding areas. The white boarding and hung tiles are hardly traditional to the area but they do give a jaunty seaside feeling. The square itself measures 17 metres across and is entered from narrow alleyways which link on to the surrounding lanes. The development contains shops and residential accommodation and provides car parking in an underground basement.

2F Brighton Square.

2G The Cricketers
Black Lion Street
The history of this pub can be traced back to the 17th century when it was known as 'The Last and Fishcart', though the present buildings date from the early 19th century. A last was a measure of 10,000 fish, and in those days the pub served the fishing community. This part of town was known as the Hempshares: hemp was prepared here for the manufacture of fishing nets and rope. However, in 1790 the Landlord was a keen cricketer and it was he who gave the pub its present name. The pub yard was used as the town's pound during the 19th century and it is recorded that in 1887 a flock of sheep was kept there while the shepherd sobered up! The pub retains a good old-fashioned interior.

2G and 2H Black Lion Street.

2H The Deryk Carver
Black Lion Street
The Deryk Carver stands on the site of the Black Lion Brewery from which the street got its name. Carver was a Protestant Martyr who was burned at Lewes in 1554. The present building is a replica of an earlier building and was built in 1974 by the architects Wells-Thorpe and Suppel. Its predecessor was thought to be quite typical of a building type which prevailed in the Lanes, and though the age of the superstructure was uncertain, the foundations date back to the mid 16th century.

2K Friends Meeting House.

2J Prince Albert Street

Prince Albert Street performs a curving diagonal cut from Market Street across Black Lion Street to Ship Street and is therefore unusual in this part of Brighton and slightly out of character with the rest of the Lanes. In fact it was carved out during the early part of the last century. The house on the corner with Meeting House Lane is a fine example of a brick front dating from around 1820. It has 5 bays on 3 storeys with an imposing central Tuscan porch. Further along is a fine trio of mid-victorian shop fronts in decorated terra cotta with delicate shop window mullions and beyond them, set back from the street, the Friends Meeting House (2K). This site was bought by the Quakers in 1806. The main wing dates from 1876 and is known as the Meeting House, while the northern block is referred to as the Institution.

2L The Elim Free Church
Union Street

The Elim Free Church or Four Square Gospel Tabernacle dominates the north side of Union Street. An earlier chapel was built on the site in 1683 but this was rebuilt in 1825 by Amon Wilds. The building has a strangely monumental and formal facade for such a narrow lane. The projecting central section is in three bays framed by Doric pilasters which support a triglyph frieze under a plain pediment. Symmetrical entrances are placed in balancing side bays. The three main windows and the doorways have been given a strong taper which serves to magnify the scale of the composition within its confined environment. After such an introduction the interior is surprisingly intimate in scale. Pews are arranged in semicircles on a raked floor around a central pulpit with additional seating provided on an upper balcony.

2J Prince Albert Street.

2L The Elim Free Church.

2M Dukes Lane
Dukes Lane runs from Ship Street to Middle Street, and is a totally new creation, having been built in 1979. The scheme was designed by the firm of Stone, Toms and Partners, and employs a mixture of Regency and Victorian elements, some of them new, some of them salvaged.

2M Dukes Lane.

2N Brighton Hippodrome
Middle Street
This building is one of Brighton's most interesting architectural curiosities. It was opened originally in 1897 as an ice rink but ice skating did not prove to be a popular pastime and in 1900 it was converted into a theatre by the great theatre architect Frank Matcham. The design was one of Matcham's finest, and much of the original work still exists, though the building was long since converted into a Bingo Hall. The street elevation is stuccoed but the original glass canopy has been removed. The auditorium is oval shaped under an enormous richly decorated dome. The Hippodrome was a variety theatre during the Great Age of Music Hall, and many famous artists played there: Sarah Bernhardt, Lillie Langtry, Charlie Chaplin, Harry Houdini. Lawrence Olivier made his debut at the Brighton Hippodrome and fell over at his first entrance.

2P The Synagogue.

2P The Synagogue
Middle Street
The new synagogue in Middle Street was the subject of a competition in 1874. Strangely no Jewish architects entered and the winning design was made by Thomas Lainson. The front is vaguely Byzantine and uses a light yellow Chichester brick. The window arches are picked out with blue and red tiles and the openings are punctuated with Corinthian pillars. The interior seats a congregation of 300 under its lofty dome.

3 THE STEINE & THE LEVEL

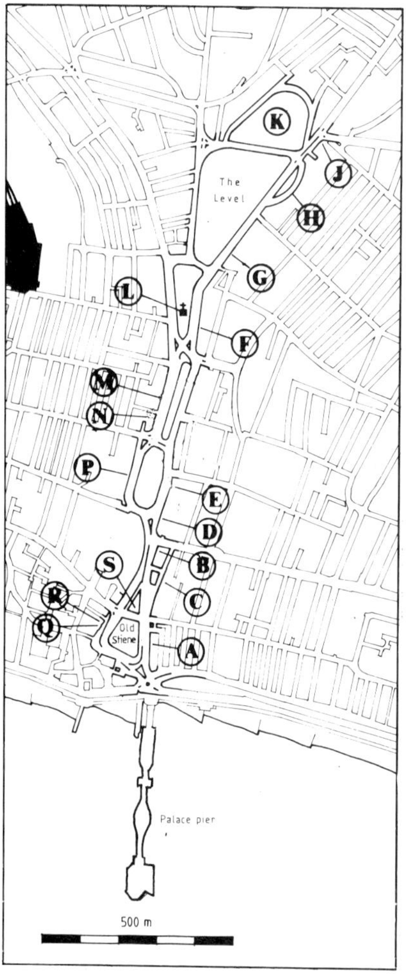

In former times the town was bounded on its eastern edge by the Steine, an area of low-lying common land beneath which flowed an underground stream known as the Wellsbourne. The waterlogged state of the ground had prevented its use for building and it served mainly as a pasture and drying ground for fishing nets. After 1750, as Brighton's popularity as a spa and holiday resort grew, the Steine became a fashionable promenade in preference to the seafront cliffs which were both windy and unsafe. In 1786 the Prince of Wales established himself in the farmhouse which fronted onto the Steine and which he eventually transformed into his Royal Pavilion. The land to either side of the Steine was quickly developed to provide fashionable accommodation for the London Society which now flocked to Brighton in the Season, while the Steine itself was fenced off and manicured. At this time a wooden sewer, Brighton's first, was built to improve drainage and to the north a cricket field and pleasure gardens were established on what later came to be known as the Level.

The name 'Steine' is of Scandinavian origin, from the world 'staene' — meaning a place of stones. In 1823 workmen digging a trench for a new gas main discovered a number of sarsen stones, blocks of grey sandstone deposited perhaps by glaciers. In 1846 they were incorporated into the base of the Victoria Fountain, a delightful water feature supported by three intertwined dolphins which was placed at the centre of the Steine by Amon Henry Wilds. This motif has since been used as the Brighton Coat of Arms.

Today the Level is the meeting point of the main roads from London and Lewes and the noble Steine has become nothing more than a giant traffic island across which the pedestrian must hop on a series of disconnected crossings.

3 The Steine Fountain.

3A 26 The Old Steine.

3A Old Steine
Building on the east side of the Steine began in the 1780s quickly blocking views from the Royal Pavilion to open countryside.

On the southern end of Victoria Gardens there are some excellent examples of Georgian town houses. No. 3 Old Steine (c 1790), is a rare example of an unchanged house. It has three

3 Holland's Marine Pavilion on the Steine.

storeys and is cobbled with brick dressings. Amon Henry Wilds refronted several houses in the Old Steine to designs by Busby during the 1820s. Of these, Nos. 23 and 26 are the most conspicuous with their full-width bow-fronts and Doric porches. Both date from the 1820s; the curved front of No. 23 is surmounted by a dentilled cornice with balustraded parapet in front of the 3rd floor windows, and with a further cornice and solid parapet above the 4th floor. No. 26, which is stuccoed with a rusticated ground floor, has imposing fluted pilasters with Ammonite capitals. This form was invented by George Dance and was used by Amon Wilds as a pun on his own Christian name. It became a family trademark after he first used it at Castle Place in Lewes (see 17K).

3B Nos. 3-4 Pavilion Parade.

3B Pavilion Parade

These tall Regency houses at the northern end of Victoria Gardens form a variegated collection of verandas, iron balconies and doorways with bróken pediments. Nos. 3-4 retain original fronts, cobbled and tarred in true rustic fashion, with painted brick dressings and quoins. No. 5 was refronted by Busby and Wilds in the 1820s and has a fine iron balcony with hood and wooden uprights. It was recently restored in full Regency flavour with shell motifs, domed ceilings, marble fire-places and hand carved doors.

3C The Parochial Offices.

3C The Parochial Offices
Princes Street

The site was originally occupied by the Old County Court Offices and was bought in 1891 by the Brighton Guardians for the sum of £5,500. The Parochial Offices were opened in 1894 and were first used for the registration of births, marriages and deaths. Later they also housed a Poor Rate Collector's Office. The highly decorated facade of red brick with stone dressings under a tiled roof with a terracotta ridge is a typical example of a Victorian public building.

3D The Liverpool Victoria Insurance Offices.

3D Grand Parade
A delightful collection of early 19th Century town houses, many of which are attributed to Wilds and Busby (notably Nos. 9, 10, 14, 18 and 19) and date from the period 1822-30. They show the characteristic wooden hooded balconies, three-light bow windows, Doric pilasters and mathematical tiles on a timber structure. The Liverpool Victoria Insurance Offices at No. 47 were probably designed by Sir Charles Barry in 1840. Here the glazing bars are intact on the first and second floors but the facade is spoilt by a more recent shop front. The whole terrace provides an attractive Georgian stage-set reinterpretation of classical motifs.

3E Faculty of Art and Design.

3E Faculty of Art and Design — Brighton Polytechnic Grand Parade
Following Government approval of the Brighton Development Plan in 1958 the large Victorian buildings which occupied the northern half of Grand Parade were demolished. A new art school was proposed and the name of Le Corbusier was put forward as its architect. However, this was not taken up and the new buildings were designed by Percy Billington, Brighton's Borough Architect, and were opened in 1967. It is arguably one of the most successful modern buildings in the town: the main facade takes on the gentle concave curve of the road and the fenestration pays respect to its bow-fronted Georgian neighbours. Sadly the rear elevation makes for a less satisfactory companion!

3F 16-18 Richmond Terrace.

3F 16-18 Richmond Terrace
St. Peters House is a very recent office addition to the Steine. It was designed by Philip Andrews of the Hibbert Andrews Partnership and completed in the summer of 1986. The motley collection of Regency buildings which stood on the site were to have been renovated, but varying floor levels and an unsound timber structure forced a decision to rebuild. This gave an opportunity to remodel the facade to read as one building while still acknowledging the former

irregularity. The pedimented left side has been rebuilt as the original, but with a mansard roof addition referencing with dormers the window pattern beneath. The right hand side balances the horizontality of the left with a strong vertical element capped by a diamond window. The narrow central section contains the main entrance and is adorned with a scallop motif crafted in plaster. This is a sensitive infill which tries to avoid banal pastiche or facsimile reproduction.

3G Nos. 4-6 Richmond Terrace.

3G Richmond Terrace

Richmond Terrace was built by Amon Henry Wilds as a series of speculative developments after 1818. Starting from the south the first houses form a pleasing succession of generous bow-fronts with stuccoed rustications to the piano nobile and basement and plain yellow brickwork above. Nos. 4-6 share a common recessed entry and seem at one time to have been one house. They were occupied by Lord Chancellor, Lord Combermere from 1826 and were visited by King George IV, a fact which is recorded on the facade by the addition of crowns to the lamp brackets. Again the piano nobile has stuccoed rustication while on the upper floor is formed by cornices and punctured by semi-circular lunette windows. No. 7 is a strangely compressed two-storey residence. Nos. 8-10 have long since disappeared having been replaced by the imposing red-brick mass of the Brighton Technical College. Beyond, Nos. 11-13 form a terrace on 2 storeys with an attic, and Nos. 14 and 15 complete the terrace. North of Southover Street Wilds collaborated with Busby to build two villas. The first, No. 16 Richmond Terrace, is framed by Doric pilasters, while the second contains a pair of houses behind a twinned porch.

3H Hanover Crescent

The Crescent was the dream of Henry Brooker, a well-known businessman and entrepreneur. He saw that a great fortune was to be made from property developing as a result of the Prince of Wales' patronage of the town. The land which was in the Islingword Furlong was divided into separately owned strips known as paulpieces. Ignoring its relative distance away from the fashionable Steine, Brooker brought the land owners together in 1814 and employed Amon Henry Wilds to create a unified development behind a single facade. By 1822 the facade was finished and the house shells were sold off to individuals who then completed the interiors to their personal requirements.

With the exception of Nos. 16 and 17, the houses stand in blocks of three, each block having its own unique combination of pilaster and capital. Sadly the original integrity of these villas has been compromised by the addition of incongruous attics. The tarred cobble wall beside the main road is a survivor of the original development.

3H Hanover Crescent.

3J Percy and Wagner Almshouses.

3J Percy and Wagner Almshouses
Adjoining Hanover Crescent to the north, these two-storey brick houses are the only surviving almshouses in Brighton. The six central houses date back to 1795 and must therefore have been the only buildings in the valley at that time. The three at each end were added in 1859 by the vigorous Vicar of Brighton, the Rev. H. M. Wagner. They have unusual pointed windows, and the two centre doorways are bracketed in an ogee-shaped head.

3K Park Crescent
The Prince Regent was a keen supporter of the cricket matches which were held on the Level on land which Thomas Read Kemp, the Lord of the Manor, granted to the inhabitants of the town for their recreation. In 1822 Kemp leased the northernmost part, now separated by Union Road, to Mr. James Ireland who opened Ireland's Pleasure Gardens which included a maze, theatre and saloon. This venture was not a success and the land was finally developed for housing by Amon Henry Wilds from 1849 onwards.

Wilds, nearing the end of his career, put forward possibly his most ambitious scheme: a 'horseshoe' crescent of 48 houses, contrived on the outside of the curve to appear as a single terrace and on the inside as a string of 24 linked villas. The form was doubtless intended to create a stop to the Level but the intrusion of Union Road provoked the construction of a boundary wall which effectively cut off the Crescent.

Designed in the Italian spirit so popular after 1830, the Crescent reveals Wilds's ingenuity in the way he treats the junctions between houses of differing heights: the villa forms are linked by three storey towers capped with heavily modelled gables, the eaves being supported on Wilds's characteristic bracket and medallion motif.

3K Park Crescent.

3L St. Peter's Church
In the 1820s a competition was held to select a design for a new church on the Level which would serve as a chapel-of-ease to the Parish Church of St. Nicholas. The winning architect was Charles Barry, much to the annoyance of the local duo of Busby and Wilds who had expected to get the commission.

The foundation stone was laid in 1825 and the church was consecrated in 1828. In 1873 it became the Parish Church. It is a large yet delicate church designed with pinnacles and buttresses in the Perpendicular Gothic style. Barry later regretted the absence of the spire which he had originally designed to cap the tower. But in spite of this omission this is one of his most important buildings and one of the first and finest of the Gothic Revival churches. Here Barry used Gothic with the serenity and purity of the Classical spirit. The three-sided apsidal chancel was replaced in 1906 by Somers Clarke, but as it was not built in a matching Portland stone it has weathered differently. A recording of the peel of ten bells, the heaviest being over one and a quarter tons, rings out over the Pacific at St. Peters, Del Mar, California. Barry went on to design St. Andrew's Church, Hove, in a completely different manner.

3L St. Peter's Church.

3M The Astoria
Gloucester Place

The Astoria on Gloucester Place was the brainchild of Brighton's cinema magnate, Councillor E. E. Lyons. The building was designed in 1933 by a Mr. E. A. Stone and, described at the time as a new departure in cinema entertainment. It was a 2,000 seat super-cinema built with a brick structure behind a handsome 45 metre long, stone faced elevation which overlooked the Steine. The interiors were simple and avoided the tawdry fripperies, meaningless luxuries and extravagances that had served only to distract previous generations of filmgoers. It was claimed to have the finest projection of picture and sound in the provinces, being equipped

3L Drawing of St. Peter's by Somers Clarke, Jnr.

with Western Electric's wide-range apparatus, and was one of the first cinemas outside London to be able to screen CinemaScope pictures. The front facade relies mainly on proportion to achieve a sense of spacious grandeur while also avoiding gratuitous decoration. Sadly it has been converted into the inevitable Bingo Hall!

3M The Astoria.

3N TSB Offices
Gloucester Place

This office development, designed by Christopher Beaver Associates, was completed in 1985. Conceived originally as a general speculative development it was adjusted at the last minute to meet the specific brief of the Trustees Savings Bank. It occupies a prominent and sensitive corner site on the west side of the Steine and has been generally welcomed as a modest and polite neighbour with its projecting window motif respecting Brighton's traditional bay windows.

3N The TSB Offices.

3P The King and Queen Pub
Marlborough Place

In 1779, a farmhouse on the western edge of the Steine was granted a licence to serve alcohol to the local agricultural community. Its popularity increased when the cricket matches on the Level were instituted, and it later prospered from an illicit trade with the neighbouring army barracks through a secret rear hatch still visible today. The Brighton Corn Market was held in the building before being moved in 1868 to the Royal Pavilion Riding House, which became known as the Corn Exchange. The inn's name originally referred to George III and Queen Charlotte. During the 1930s the architects Clayton and Black rebuilt the pub as an elaborate Tudoresque facsimile with an impressive array of seemingly authentic details: tapestries and heraldic glass, carved oak timbers and linen-fold panelpieces. The Brighton Herald stated that:

> It is something more than a handsome, spacious building, wherein people can eat, drink, and be merry in perfect comfort. It is a gorgeous flight of architectural imagination.

At the same time the original Royal Couple were replaced by the more appropriate Henry VIII and Anne Boleyn!

3Q Marlborough House
Old Steine (West)

The original house was built for one Samuel Shergold, a proprietor of the Castle Hotel, in 1769. Two years later he sold it to the fourth Duke of Marlborough who gave it his name before selling it on to William 'Single Speech'

3Q Marlborough House.

Hamilton in 1786. Hamilton then employed Robert Adam to remodel the house and to reface the brick front in 'Adam's Artificial Stone'. The result which we see today is a simple composition of five bays on two storeys. The outer bays project under plain pediments and are given 'Serliana' windows at the ground floor. The entrance occupies the centre bay and is punctuated by delicate Roman Doric Columns. The plain walls and simple pattern of openings appealed to Pevsner who declared it to be the finest facade in Brighton!

3P King and Queen Pub.

3R Steine House
Old Steine (West)

Steine House was built by William Porden in 1804 for Mrs. Fitzherbert, the clandestine wife of the Prince of Wales. It was substantially remodelled in 1864 and an interior staircase is the sole surviving element from the original design.

3S War Memorial

The War Memorial was designed in 1921 by J. W. Simpson, a former President of the RIBA. It was formally unveiled in the following year by Earl Beatty, Admiral of the Fleet, at a ceremony attended by Mayor and Corporation in full robes.

4 THE NORTH LAINE

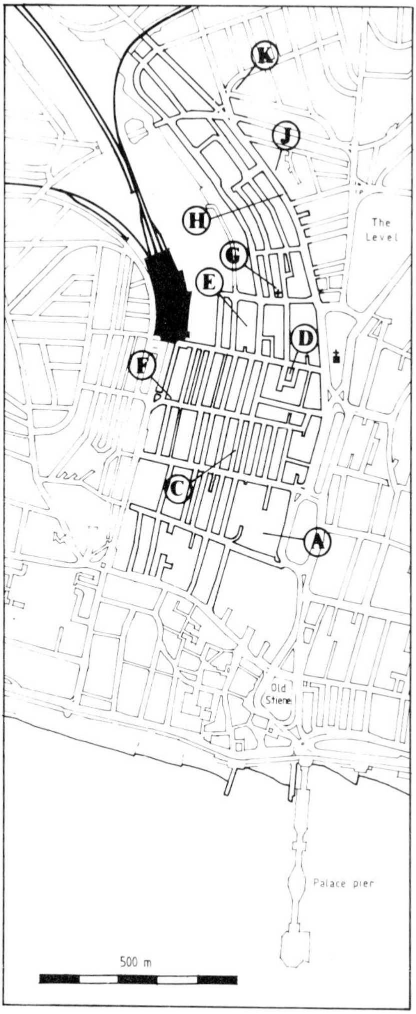

Visitors to Brighton are often confused by the word "laine". The area known as "The Lanes" derives from its many narrow alleyways. However, the word "laine" is derived from the Saxon word "laen" meaning gift or loan, and refers to an area of farmland. The old town of Brighton was encircled by five laines, each of which was divided into broad tracts known as furlongs and further divided into strips known as paul-pieces. Individual landowners in the town might own paul-pieces in a number of locations, and rarely were adjoining paul-pieces owned by the same person. During the mid-eighteenth century the increasing popularity of Brighton as a resort led to new building development within the core of the old town, in the nearby Steine, and out into the adjacent laines. The North Laine lay immediately to the north of the old town and development spread into it after 1770. Land could only be obtained as and when paul-pieces were put on the market by their owners. In the case of the North Laine the paul-pieces ran north-south and measured typically 8 metres by 50 metres. The farming strip became the unit of building development, and, the street system which grew up became a fossil representation of the earlier field system. The original furlongs had been separated by tracks known as "leakways" and these became the principle streets running from east to west: Church Street, North Road, Gloucester Road and Trafalgar Street. The paul-pieces developed as terraces with streets running from north to south at approximately 32 metre intervals: Regent Street, Gardner Street, Tichborne Street, Bread Street, etc.

Development of the North Laine started with North Row, now Marlborough Place, which was built overlooking the Steine in what was the most easterly paul-piece of the "Home Furlong" in 1772. Wealthy tradespeople built substantial houses along the entire eastern border of the Laine as far as Preston Circus, a few of them can still be seen behind the shop fronts of London Road. However, the interior of the Laine was developed mainly with workshops, shops and working class housing, much of it two storeyed with a very particular grain and scale.

During the post-war period the North Laine was seen as an area ripe for redevelopment and a downward spiral of confidence and condition set in. As recently as 1973 the planning consultants Wilson and Womersley were making proposals in the Brighton Central Area Study which would have resulted in the virtual extinction of the North Laine as a place in which to live and work, and its transformation into an area through which motor cars could move freely and be parked in vast numbers. Hugh Wilson received a knighthood and became President of the RIBA while the North Laine came to look more and more like a bomb site. Fortunately the plans of the seventies were shelved in response to new economic realities. This has meant that, on the one hand, a number of cleared sites have remained permanently derelict and continue to provide cheap parking spaces for non rate-paying commuters from out of town, while on the other, several streets have enjoyed something of a renaissance. There is now an active North Laine Community Association which guards the interests of residents.

4A The Regent Swimming Pool
Church Street

The block of land contained by Church Street, Regent Street, North Road and Marlborough Place did not develop according to the classic paul-piece pattern. The paul-pieces behind Malborogh Place were acquired compulsorily at the end of the 18th century for the building of army barracks. In the 19th century these were replaced by public swimming baths. During the 1970s the whole block was identified in the Brighton Central Area Study as a site to be redeveloped for offices, a library, a swimming pool and some housing. A detailed redevelopment proposal involving Brighton Council with a private developer was approved in 1974 but to date

4A Entrance to the Regent swimming pool.

the new Regent Swimming Pool is the only piece of the jig-saw puzzle to have been put in place. The pool was designed by the Brighton Borough Architect's Department and was completed in 1981 at a cost of £2.5 million. It is a good example of modern swimming pool design with excellent facilities housed in a successful interior. The external form, however, is still waiting for the rest of the jig-saw and it lies like some great red brick whale marooned in a sea of parked cars. New redevelopment proposals are now on the table and it seems possible that the pool will one day be joined by an ice rink, a glazed mall a library and an office complex.

4C Kensington Gardens

This narrow cobbled pedestrian street gets its name from the market gardens which grew up on the fringe of the North Laine at the end of the 18th century. It is currently enjoying a new lease of life as a link in the chain of shopping streets which run down through the North Laine from London Road to Bond Street. Part of its popularity is perhaps due to its intimate scale, and to the absence of motor cars.

4D Pelham Square
Trafalgar Street

Pelham Square is one of the very few inland squares of Brighton, and is something of an oddity in the North Laine's grid of streets. It is thought that it arose quite accidentally, and that its component sides were built quite separately after 1820.

4D Pelham Square.

4E Theobald House
Whitecross Street
Theobald House is the consequence of the Corbusian dream of towers in a park. Sadly, in this case the park turns out to be for motor cars! Built in 1966 the brick tower contains 110 flats in groups of 6 per floor on 18 floors. Here was a brave attempt to sweep away the mean and over-crowded terraces of the North Laine and replace them with modern, light and airy homes. Today the tide of opinion has turned and Theobald House, along with its contemporaries in other parts of the town, is perceived as a monument to Municipal Landlordism, a gaunt tower out of sympathy and scale with its surroundings, a dream turned to nightmare.

4E Theobald House.

4F Office Building
Frederick Place/Gloucester Road
This small office development by the architects Hughes, Lomax and Adutt, occupies a tricky corner site and demonstrates that a modern building can be knitted into an existing urban fabric without resorting to pastiche. There are three main elements: a corner block of three storeys, a linking tower containing vertical circulation and a main block containing the office accommodation on five storeys. Looking down from the Queen's Road Quadrant it can be seen how these three elements are used to reconcile the conflicting scales of two streets. The dark patterned brickwork and the simple window openings achieve a pleasing harmony.

4F Office Building, Frederick Place.

4G St. Bartholomew's Church
Anne Street
St. Bartholomew's is certainly one of Brighton's most impressive and moving churches. It was commissioned by the Reverend Arthur Wagner and designed by a little-known local architect called Edmund Scott. The initial building phase lasted from 1872 to 1874. Scott's first design was for a long, narrow and relatively low church. Work had already started on site, however, when Wagner called a halt to demand something more grand. In the final design the height of the nave was more than doubled: the wallplate is 27 metres above the floor and the ridge plate 42 metres. St. Bartholomew's nave is 1 metre higher than Westminster Abbey's and is the highest of any parish church in the land, its overall dimensions being based on those given in the Bible for Noah's Ark. St. Bartholomew's was one of a number of Brighton churches in which the teachings of the Oxford Movement were supported. The church aroused strong opposition, partly because of its design and partly because of

the supposed popish sympathies of its patron. At a Council debate in 1893 it was described variously as "a cheese warehouse", "Noah's Ark in brick", "a monster excrescence", "uselessly large", "painfully ugly and sadly out of place" and as "Wagner's folly". Few buildings in Brighton have encountered such opposition!

Wagner's aim had been to provide maximum magnificence at minimal cost. Built to its great height using stock bricks with the barest of ornament, St. Bartholomew's was claimed to have been the cheapest church per cubic metre of all time!

The interior consists of a nave with 9 shallow side chapels formed out of nothing more than buttresses. The decorations were added between 1895 and 1910 by Henry Wilson, a pupil of Sedding, and are probably much richer than Scott had intended. However, the use of marbles and chalk, reminiscent of Westminster Cathedral, is most impressive. The baldacchino is 14 metres high and was erected in 1900 to Wilson's design. The church is used regularly today for orchestral concerts.

4G St. Bartholomew's Church.

4H London Road

As its name implies, London Road was and is the main route out of Brighton towards London. It was developed with fairly substantial houses, many of them residences of successful tradespeople, during the early

4G St. Bartholomew's: Interior.

years of the 19th century. Today it is lined with shops and supermarkets, though in places the original houses can still be seen several metres back from the line of the shop fronts at first floor level. Brighton's only open market, a rather scruffy affair, lies between London Road and the Level. St. Peter's Vicarage (4J) on the east side of London Road at No. 87 dates from 1825 and has been attributed to Busby and Wilds. A handsome front, 3 bays with rusticated ground floor and double height Ionic pilasters, it now looks a little lost in its surroundings. Further north, at Preston Circus, is the Duke of York's cinema (4K). This was opened in 1910 by Mrs. Violet Melnotte-Wyatt and was Brighton's first "Electric Bioscope". Although it is a little battered today, it still looks much as it must have done 77 years ago, and it still functions as a cinema!

4K Duke of York's Cinema.

5 NORTH STREET, WEST STREET & QUEEN'S ROAD

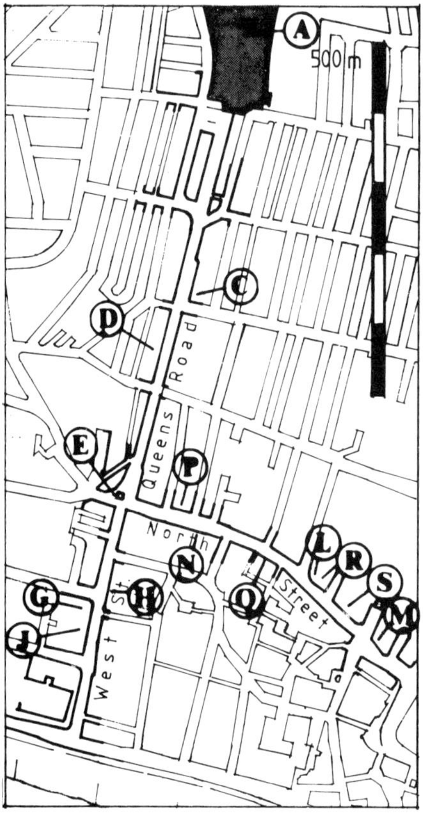

Here are three streets which are strangely disconnected from the areas through which they pass. North Street, once the northernmost street of the old town, acts as a frontier between the North Laine and the Lanes and belongs to neither of them. Likewise West Street forms the western edge of the old town but it guards its own distinctive character. Queen's Road was cut through an existing area in order to link the railway station to the centre. All three streets meet at the Clock Tower from which a fourth short street links with the beginnings of Western Road, Brighton's main shopping street, and Dyke Road. Queen's Road and West Street ought to offer the visitor newly arrived by train, a fine promenade to the sea-front. Sadly, however, Queen's Road is now looking very run down and modern developments have destroyed the integrity of West Street. The pedestrian soon realises that Brighton is a town in which junctions are arranged to suit the convenience of the motorist and nowhere is this more apparent than at the Clock Tower where the three streets meet.

5A Brighton Railway Station
Queen's Road

5A The Original Station.

The coming of the railway to Brighton was preceded by much bitter argument. When a rail link with London was first mooted in 1825 there were many who were totally opposed to the whole notion. Later the argument centred on the location of the terminus and the choice of route. In 1835 the townsfolk declared themselves in favour of Stephenson's line with a terminus in Shoreham, but in the following year a government enquiry found in favour of Sir John Rennie's direct line. Rennie's original plan would have placed the terminus on what was then the Hanover Cricket Ground and is now Park Crescent (see 3K), but in the final scheme the terminus was located above the North Laine. The line to London finally opened in September 1841.

The terminus building was designed by David Mocatta, architect to the London and Brighton Railway Company, and a student of Sir John Soane. Mocatta also designed most of the intermediate stations and bridges on the line. In its original form the terminus

5A The Station Concourse.

building was a handsome composition in the Italian Villa style with a central arcade entrance behind a Tuscan colonnade. The volume of traffic grew very quickly with the opening of branch lines to Shoreham and Lewes and by 1850 there were 50 trains per day coming into Brighton. In 1882 it became necessary to replace the original train sheds and H. E. Wallis designed the present single span arched roof. This is a typically elegant Victorian train shed of glass and iron with delicate dolphin designs on the spandrels between the main arches. At the same time Mocatta's colonnade was removed and his facade was mutilated and hidden behind the ugly porte cochere which remains to this day.

5B Queen's Road

Queen's Road was driven through an area of slum housing known as Petty France to create a link from the railway station to West Street and the seafront beyond. The final link to the station forecourt involved the construction of a bridge over Trafalgar Street. For the day trippers it offered a first prospect of the sea as they trooped from their trains towards the beaches. Today's visitors must first negotiate a busy taxi rank and a bus terminus and their first view of Brighton is far from encouraging.

The upper section of Queen's Road is in a very neglected state: No. 5 on the east side has been empty for several years and now has small saplings growing from its cornice! Further down at the junction with North Street is Sun Dial House (5C), built in 1896 and named after the large sun dial which can still be seen today on the south-facing elevation under the warning: "Our days on earth are as a shadow and there are none abiding". No. 25 on the other side, an ungainly pile with a central bay window hanging over a recessed Doric porch, is thought to be an early building from the partnership of Busby and Wilds and is now used as the Masonic Temple (5D).

5C Sun Dial House.

5E The Clock Tower

5E The Clock Tower as seen from Queen's Road.

The Clock Tower stands at the junction of Queen's Road, North Street, West Street and Western Road, and was built in 1887 by a local advertising magnate called John Willing and his architect John Johnson to commemorate Queen Victoria's Jubilee. Described by Pevsner as 'worthless' and by others as a 'giant saltcellar' it is in fact a charmingly ugly piece of Victorian baroque. At its base are four porticos each one framing the medallion portrait of a royal personage. Four carved boats point the visitor variously towards the sea, Hove, the station and Kemp Town. Above its copper dome is a small copper sphere on a shaft which used to raise itself up and down hydraulically at each hour in response to an electrical signal from Greenwich. The Victorians exercised few scruples when it came to combining utility with beauty and, as well as telling the time, pointing the way, and framing royal portraits, the Clock Tower manages to incorporate public lavatories beneath its base. Today it is rather lost in a jumble of modern street furniture, the visitors are too preoccupied with the business of negotiating a dangerously confusing junction to spare it their attention.

5F West Street

West Street marks what was once the western limit of the old town. When Brighton first came into fashion as a resort it was the area near to the Steine which found favour with visitors and the western part of the town housed a more local community. At this time West Street was lined with small shops and unpretentious dwellings beside open fields. The street was widened in the 1820s and the original houses were replaced on the west side by Victorian development. Today a few 18th century houses survive on the east side and the Victorian houses have all but disappeared. The street is subdued by the massive Churchill Square and Brighton Centre Developments which loom behind its western side. No. 77 is an interesting survivor, a double fronted house with generous bows now used as a restaurant.

5G Abbey National Building Society West Street

5G The view down West Street.

The office building now occupied by the Abbey National Building Society was built in 1938 to designs by the architect H. E. Mendelssohn, and not, as is sometimes thought, by Eric Mendelsohn. In fact the entrance is placed on a curving corner in a manner vaguely reminiscent of the architect's expressionist namesake, though the bold design has been diluted by recent alterations and the original curved glass windows have been filled in. An inscription on one of the stone panels reads: "Built 1938 H. E. Mendelssohn".

5H "The Nellie Peck"
West Street

This pub started life as 'The Compasses' and was later known as 'The Carpenters Arms'. The present long bar configuration was installed in 1925. The exuberant facade with its eagles and mermaids has recently been renovated and aptly painted in gay colours. At the rear of the bar an interesting stained glass window depicts the West Pier.

5H "The Nellie Peck".

5J St. Paul's Church
West Street

This remarkable church was built originally to serve the poorer communities living in the western part of the old town, and was the first in Brighton to promote the teachings of the Oxford Movement which called for a Catholic revival within the Church of England. Money for the building was raised by Henry Michell Wagner and the first vicar was his son Arthur Wagner. The original building was designed by Richard Cromwell Carpenter and was

5J St. Paul's Church as it was originally designed.

constructed between 1846 and 1848. The church has conventional west-east orientation and the sanctuary faces onto West Street. The narthex was added to the west end by Bodley in 1887 and a long, gloomy passageway built by Denman runs along the entire south wall to connect it with the pavement. Unusually for a church in Brighton, the walls are built from knapped flint with limestone quoins. The tower was to have had a stone spire but the present timber spire was added by Carpenter's son in 1873. This formed a major landmark and was used as a beacon by sailors, but today it is dwarfed by newer buildings such as Sussex Heights (10E). The first impression of the interior is one of extreme simplicity. The quatrefoil piers and plain arches are painted white in contrast with the steep black roof with its arched braces.

Carpenter's original wooden pulpit is on the left while to the right is a magnificent brass lectern representing the Angels of the Apocalypse. The high altar is separated from the nave by a timber screen designed originally by Carpenter but later embellished by Bodley. The original altar triptych by Burne-Jones is now in the Brighton Museum. The stained glass windows in the church are by Pugin and those in the narthex are by Kempe.

5K North Street

5L A view down North Street showing the Leeds Permanent.

North Street originally formed the northern edge of the town, separating it from the farm strips of the North Laine. Today it is a busy commercial street dividing the picturesque maze of the Lanes from the grid of streets which later grew up on the North Laine. As a street it lacks any consistency of style or scale and is made up of a mixed bag of buildings from different periods. The north side is dominated by banks and building societies, the south by the long front of Hannington's Store. Barclay's Bank at the corner of King's Place, dates surprisingly from the 1950s while Midland and the National Westminster, glowering at each other across the entrance to Bond Street, are leftover examples of Edwarian baroque built in the 1920s.

The Leeds Permanent Building Society (5L) on the corner of New Road is an example of Edwardian baroque at its best: a confident composition in delicate pink granite. It was designed by Clayton and Black in 1904. A second National Westminster Bank on the corner of Pavilion Buildings (5M) was designed in 1911 by Godfrey Pinkerton. This is more restrained than its banking brothers and shows some fine relief carving. North Street offers its own permutation of the standard High Street shop fronts with their plastic logos. The Body Shop (5N) in the middle of the south side is an example of a packaging style which embraces everything from the soap it sells to the shop fittings and is interesting because it was an early branch of what has now become a national chain.

5K Midland Bank.

5P Ladbroke's Bingo Hall North Street

The present Bingo Hall started life as the Essoldo Cinema. Its interiors were designed in the mid 1930s by J. Alexandra in early Art Deco style and the facade bears a trace of Moderne. It was converted to a Bingo Hall in 1964.

5Q The Regency Building Society
North Street
This office building was originally built in 1785 as a coaching inn. It was first called "The New Inn", but in 1830 it was renamed "The Clarence Hotel" when the Duke of Clarence became William IV. The main block contained 26 bedrooms as well as a coffee room and various sitting rooms while the rear yards had accommodation for 50 horses and 6 coaches. The front elevation has a classical severity which has been carefully restored by the present owners and it is the best surviving building of its period in the street. The main entrance to the offices is by means of a proud Tuscan porch with iron railings and a short flight of steps leading to double doors under a semi-circular fanlight. To its left a shop front has been neatly inserted into the wall behind four Tuscan pilasters and succeeds in balancing the original coach entrance on the right.

5Q The New Inn 1830.

5R The Chapel Royal
North Street
The foundation stone of the Chapel Royal was laid by the Prince Regent in 1793 and the building was completed in 1795 to designs by Thomas Saunders. It was originally intended to serve as a Chapel of Ease to St. Nicholas taking overflow congregations during the summer months. The Prince was for several years a regular member of the congregation but a sermon on immorality upset him and in 1822, having bought the Castle Hotel, he converted its ballroom into a private chapel. At the end of the Regency Period central Brighton ceased to be a fashionable place in which to live and the Chapel Royal, having lost its wealthier parishioners, fell into disrepair. In 1876 the architect Sir Arthur Blomfield supervised repairs and added the present brick facades and clock tower. The chapel was planned originally in the form of a Greek Cross with galleries in all but the western arm. Blomfield removed the northern gallery to create a side chapel, and today the eastern arm is screened off to create a foyer and meeting room. The central cube of the chapel is lit from a square lantern in the roof.

5S Norwich Union Insurance Building
North Street

This modern office building, known as Princes House, was designed by H. S. Goodhart-Rendel in 1935, two years after he designed St. Wilfred's Church in Elm Grove (12G). Goodhart-Rendel was an eminent architect of his day who was elected President of the RIBA and who once observed that, "usefulness alone is a dreary end to man's labour". Here is, on the face of it, a modern steel-framed office building. However, the handling of the corner and the decorative treatment of the cladding materials set it apart from its contemporaries. The sand-faced handmade bricks are arranged in panels to express the structural frame and are punctuated with blue mosaic inserts.

Originally the corner entrance led through a seven sided hall to a triangular staircase lit from the rear, but this was all swept away in a rash of modernisation which also added an incongruous canopy to the front elevation.

6 THE SEASIDE

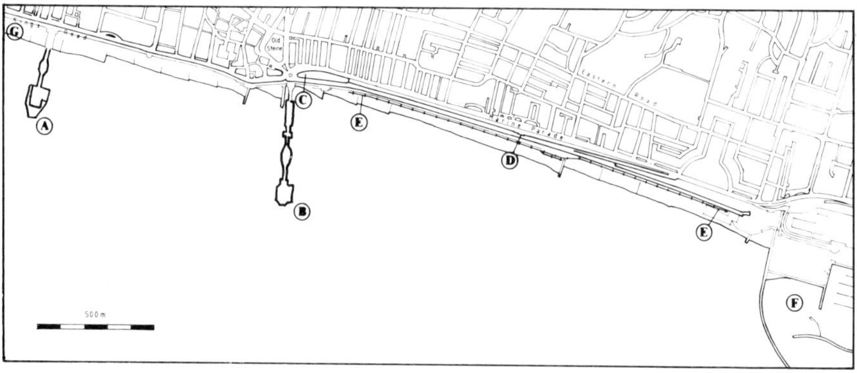

Brighton has always, in one way or another, owed its existence to the sea. First a seafaring and fishing town, its rise to prominence as a resort was as much due to Dr. Russell's promotion of the health-giving properties of its seawater as to its later patronage by the Prince Regent. Sea-bathing as a pastime seems to have developed first during the 18th century, and bathing machines, those discreet sentry boxes on wheels which could be pushed to the water's edge, made an appearance on Brighton's beaches in about 1750. At that time the cliffs had receded to the very edge of the town, threatening property. New sea defences were begun during the 1750s, and the beginnings of a sea-front road and a retaining wall were constructed at the bottom of Ship Street during the 1760s. In 1822 a new road link was built by public subscription between West Street and East Street and was opened by George IV who named it "King's Road". However, a final link to the end of the Steine was only formed in 1829 with the opening of Grand Junction Road.

Brighton's remarkable Chain Pier was built in 1823 by Captain Samuel Brown. It was located some 500 metres to the east of the entrance to the Steine and projected about 350 metres out to sea. The pier was built in four spans supported by suspension arches of chain which hung from four massive pylons. Marine Parade was in the process of being extended along the cliff-top, and a new lower road called the Esplanade was built below a massive cliff wall to give access to the new pier. The Esplanade and the cliff wall were extended eastwards as the century progressed to create what is now known as Madeira Drive. The Chain Pier led a checkered existence and was finally swept away during a heavy storm in 1896.

With the passing of the Regency, Brighton's popularity as a fashionable resort declined. However, in 1841 the rail link with London was opened and it soon became a favourite target for day trippers, eager to escape from the grime of the capital. During the present century Brighton enjoyed something of a boom between the wars, both as a commuter dormitory and as a holiday resort. The mood of the pre-war decade was captured in Graham Greene's novel 'Brighton Rock'. Since the war Brighton's popularity has been dinted by the package holiday boom, and today the conference industry has taken over from the day tripper. The seafront offers only sad reminders of its jolly past. One pier is closed and the other offers little besides an army of fruit machines. Brighton's only open air swimming pool at Black Rock was recently demolished, and the unfinished Brighton Marina is at present being partially redeveloped as a hypermarket.

Chain Pier.

6A The West Pier
Kings Road

The Brighton West Pier was designed by Eugenius Birch and built by the Brighton West Pier Company in 1863-66 at a cost of £30,000. It was one of the first piers to be built for the purpose of promenading and pleasure along with those at Deal (1863-64), Aberystwyth (1864-65), Bognor (1864-65) and Lytham (1864-65).

The design was typical of the 1860s. The original structure was of cast and wrought iron. Mild steel was used in the extension of the head in 1893 giving it a total length of 335 metres. The columns and column heads were originally of cast iron seated on wrought iron, though these have mostly been replaced in mild steel.

Since its opening in 1866 the pier has undergone many alterations. In 1890 the sea end was widened to accommodate a large pavilion and the central windscreen was added. In 1903 the pavilion was converted into a theatre in the popular oriental manner. In 1916 a concert hall was opened at the pier's centre point.

The West Pier attracted thousands of visitors each year: 600,000 people passed through its turnstiles in 1875. But like many other piers it had its share of misfortunes. In 1868 'The Times' reported panic among the promenaders when its structure oscillated under the action of wind and sea and, as a result, its popularity declined for a time. In 1896 a powerful storm destroyed the Chain Pier and debris caused serious damage to the shore end of the West Pier. During the Second World War the pier was covered with sand bags and anti-aircraft guns and suffered some damage. The pier was later bought by a private company for £100,000 and was used for the shooting of the film 'Oh What a Lovely War'. Soon after this the sea end was condemned as unsafe and was closed in 1971. Finally the shore end was closed in 1975. The pier is now owned by the West Pier Trust and work has begun on the first stage of a programme of restoration. This will include improvements to the shore end and urgent repairs to the structure.

6A The West Pier: today.

6A The West Pier: in its heyday.

6B The Palace Pier
Madeira Drive

6B The Palace Pier (c 1912).

The Palace Pier is considered to be the finest pier ever built. It was designed by R. St. Moore and was built by Arthur Mayoh of Manchester.

It was intended that the new pier should replace the old Chain Pier, built in 1822-3 by Samuel Brown and destroyed in 1896 by a violent storm. The main section of deck was opened in 1899 and, with the addition of the theatre in 1901, it became a great success. In its early days 2 million visitors passed through the turnstiles each year. This popularity was due in part to its position as a continuation of the Steine.

In 1910 the pier received a new pavilion at its shore end. Originally used as a concert hall it has now been converted into an amusement hall called the Palace of Fun.

During the Second World War part of the pier was destroyed, but it was rebuilt and re-opened by 1946.

In 1973 severe structural damage was caused by a barge which slipped its moorings. The damage was repaired by the owners of the barge and a new Helter-Skelter tower was brought from Rhyl.

Today the pier is in a bad state of repair, and its theatre in the process of being rebuilt, but it still manages to attract thousands of visitors each year.

6C The Aquarium
Madeira Drive

The Aquarium lies between Marine Parade and the Marine Drive. It was designed by Eugenius Birch who also built the West Pier. In an early design Birch incorporated a number of towers and turrets, but this was rejected because it threatened to cut off views of the sea. The final scheme was set into the cliff and incorporated a 30 metre tank containing half a million litres of water which could house dolphins and small whales. The Aquarium was opened in August 1872 and with its rooftop promenade it soon became a popular attraction.

In 1929 the Corporation began a programme of reconstruction, adding a restaurant and bandstand to the roof and improving the pumps and aeration equipment. At this time the original Clocktower was moved from the Aquarium to the entrance of the Palace Pier.

In 1967 the old ballroom, which had been added in 1931, was converted into a Dolphinarium.

6B The Palace Pier: showing the skeleton of its old theatre.

6D Madeira Drive

Madeira Terrace, which forms a broad promenade halfway up the seawall, was started in 1895. A shelter hall and hydraulic lift were added in 1896, and the whole scheme was completed in 1898. The terrace and arches enclose a covered promenade and cover a distance of ¾ mile from the Aquarium to Dukes Mound. The cast iron columns and scalloped arches were inspired by the Indian screen on the east front of the Royal Pavilion.

In 1905 Harry Preston promoted a scheme to lay Tarmac along Madeira Drive from the Palace Pier to Kemp Town a distance of nearly a mile, so that it might serve as a motor racing track. Madeira Terrace provided the ideal viewing platform. The scheme provoked strong opposition but speed trials still take place to this day, and Madeira Drive serves as the final straight of the London to Brighton Veteran Car Rally.

The Madeira Lift was designed by the Borough Surveyor, Philip C. Lockwood. The lift was originally operated by a hydraulic pump which provided a smooth and noiseless ride from Madeira Drive to Marine Parade. The shelter housing the lift carries obvious references to the Royal Pavilion with its dragons and its scaly roof.

6D The Madeira Lift.

When the Mayor of Brighton, Alderman C. Mainwaring, opened Madeira Terrace in 1890 he observed that the money spent on the project would have been better employed on extending the road to Rottingdean!

The whole Madeira Drive project with its terraces, arches, shelters, lamp-posts and seats can be viewed as a remarkable example of Victorian municipal development combining rugged utility with sprightly design.

6E Volks Railway

The Volk Electric Railway (VER), which runs from the promenade west of the Palace Pier to Black Rock and the Marina yacht basin, was the inspiration of Magnus Volk of Brighton. It was opened on 4th August 1883, to become the first public electric railway in Great Britain. The original line ran from the Aquarium to the old Chain Pier.

Soon after its completion, Volk made plans to extend it westwards, taking in the major part of Brighton seafront. However, Brighton Council refused him permission, but did allow him to extend the line eastwards. The new line finally extended as far as Paston Place, Kemp Town. It was opened on 4th April 1884 and is still in operation today.

6F Brighton Marina

The Marine Project was the inspiration of local garage-owner and yachtsman Henry Cohen. His original idea, hatched in 1963, was for a harbour with moorings for 3,000 boats to be situated on the eastern seafront between Dukes Mound and the Madeira Lift. It would have included a heliport and hovercraft station as well as flats, hotels, restaurants, conference halls and the like. The scheme met with stiff opposition and a new site was chosen to the east of Black Rock following advice from the planner Sir William Holford. The project was started but never finished. The harbour is formed by a huge breakwater made up of 110 caissons each one 12 metres high and weighing 600 tons. It enclosed 30 hectares of sheltered water, though recently the inner harbour was

6F Brighton Marina.

filled in to create a site for a projected hypermarket. The hotels and hovercrafts and heliports never materialised and the Marina stands as a half-finished monument to one man's ambition.

6G The Birdcage Bandstand
Kings Road

The Birdcage Bandstand is one of the most delightful bits of seaside furniture which grace the seafront. It was built in 1884 and was used to stage concerts before the advent of the noisy motorcar. The oriental dome is supported by an octagon of elegant arches which spring from a solid masonry platform. The delicate tracery of the balustrade and the arches is cast iron and was made in Lewes. There have been several attempts to remove this 'redundant' building. Perhaps the age of the seaside brass band concert is past, but here is a structure which continues to delight the eye if not the ear.

6G The Birdcage Bandstand.

7 EASTERN SEAFRONT

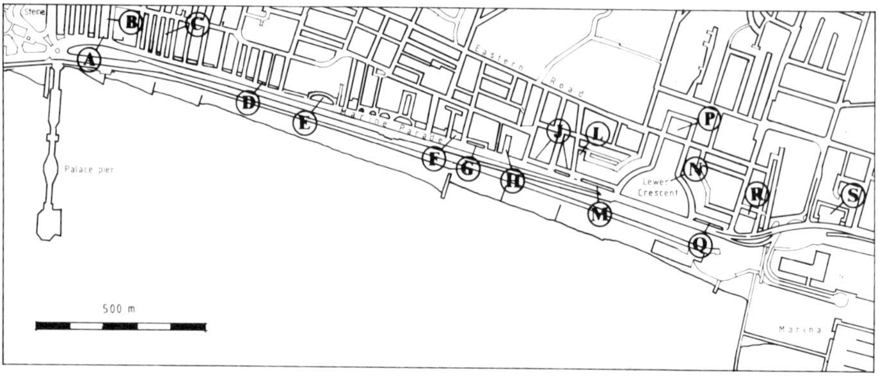

Marine Parade, once known as East Cliff, stretches from the Palace Pier to Kemp Town and was formed in 1793 as part of the Battery Defences during the Napoleonic Wars. It served as the Brighton to Rottingdean turnpike road. Development began somewhat modestly around the turn of the eighteenth century from the Steine eastwards. The oldest surviving buildings, which were lodging houses, can be found just east of the Steine in Camelford and Charles Street. The first single architectural composition of houses to be built in Brighton was commenced in 1798 at Royal Crescent, half a mile to the east.

From the Royal Crescent Hotel to Kemp Town there is to be found the greatest stretch of intact facade-scape in Brighton, dating from 1820 onwards. A large proportion of these facades were designed by the Wilds and Busby partnership and were built by Thomas Cubitt, the London builder. Many still bear the original bold character of the period. Although the elder Wilds was reserved in his use of architectural detail, his son and Charles Busby his partner were evidently influenced in their widespread use of classical orders of columns, exaggerated cornices and dentillations, shell ornament and other emphasised decoration, by contemporary architectural writers like Stuart and Revett and Robert Wood. A Piranesian approach to ancient architecture was tempered with awareness of actual measured drawings of Greek and Roman buildings.

In 1827 Brighton Council, after pressure from local residents whose buildings were close to the cliff edge, commenced the vast Marine wall project which effectively replaced the line of crumbling cliffs in front of Marine Parade. The wall was a mile and a half in length and stretched from the bottom of Middle Street to Kemp Town. It gave rise to Madeira Drive below and Marine Parade above, linked by ramps at Black Rock and Duke's mound. Brighton was thus given a splendid seafront road and promenade to which were added the arches of Madeira Terrace and the delightful range of cast-iron lampposts inspired by the Chinese lanterns of the Royal Pavilion.

7A Office Development
18 Marine Parade

18 Marine Parade is believed to have been designed by Wilds and Busby in the 1820s. It is part of a group of 19th century houses which include 20-24 Madeira Place, recently refurbished by the Miller Bourne Partnership to provide 2,600 square metres of modern lettable office space. Madeira Place was known originally as German Place until the residents forced a change of name after World War One. Research into old photographs show the Madeira Place elevation of 18 Marine Parade with a full height bow which must have preceded the later Victorian bay. Also a canopy was known to have existed on the south elevation in the early 1900s. Both have been reinstated. The facades of 20-24 Madeira Place have been rebuilt and modified to allow floors to be carried through at the same levels. Existing mouldings have been used to cast and set new ones on the new facade to maintain street profiles as accurately as possible. Whether or not it is admissible to revamp Georgian domestic buildings and use a reconstituted language as a front to speculative offices is a moot point.

7B 8-19 Camelford Street
This terrace of largely two storey lodging houses contains some of the oldest surviving buildings on the eastern seafront.

They are built of a variety of materials of which brick and render are predominant. These simple very early nineteenth century lodgings contrast with the later Neo-classic houses on the seafront with their sophisticated frontages.

7C The New Steine
A pleasing assortment of early 19th century houses set around a central private garden, intended as a major project. As so often happened in Brighton (e.g. Bedford and Regency Squares), the initial plan and control by the original developers foundered and plots were sold without effective control on the facades being enforced.

7D The Lanes Hotel.

7D The Lanes Hotel
A peculiarly inappropriate design by Colonel R. W. Edis imitating the country house manner of his friend Norman Shaw. Designed 1879-80 with knapped flints, red brick work, tile hanging and gables, it is difficult to imagine why a more urban vocabulary of the time was not used. Some years later Edis produced Marylebone Station which appears to fit in well with 18th century street architecture. Perhaps he felt an outbreak of 'Holiday Queen Anne' was justified as a one off expression here of the new style of liberty and light. A little further along the block are No. 73 and No. 74, possibly by Wilds and Busby. No. 76, the Brighton British Legion Club, is believed to be a design by Charles Barry. Nos. 73 and 80-83 are more works by Wilds and Busby, here with interesting leaf capitals.

7E Royal Crescent.

7E Royal Crescent
Royal Crescent, commissioned by J. B. Otto, a West Indian speculator, was the first single architectural composition of houses to be built in Brighton. Building began in 1798, but Otto ran into financial difficulties which caused him to return to his homeland after completing only three houses at each end of the Crescent. He succeeded in raising the necessary funds and the Crescent was completed in 1807. However, the long period over which the project was built was not unusual in Brighton. Located half a mile to the east of the Pavilion, it is a series of bay-fronted terrace houses with facades which vary only in the details of classical entrance doorways, bay windows, surrounds, balustrades and blind boxes. There is also a variation in size and internal construction. Unlike the houses of the period in Grenville Place and Bedford Square, which are respectively flint and render, they are timber-framed with brick infilling and faced with black iridescent glazed mathematical tiles, a building system used in a number of houses in Brighton and elsewhere in Sussex. Although some of the timber framed and tiled houses are not near the sea it would appear that the tiled face resists the penetration of wind-driven rain and sea-spray better than would ordinary brickwork of that period. The houses have one window and a three-light curved or canted bay on each floor. It has been suggested that the canted bays were originally bows and in

fact the first house built on the east end is bow-fronted. Comparing the bow-fronted example with those with canted bays it is not easy to discover in the details evidence of varying age and date which might support this notion.

This was speculative housing for middle class buyers and it combines vernacular construction and finishes with a few refined references to neo-classicism. The plans and sections of the houses were a modest version of houses built before 1800 on the London estates. The bonnet canopies and balconies which accentuate the first floor, the doorways which are delightfully classical some with semi-circular fanlights some with columns, entablatures and rectangular fanlights all show refinement in the choice of details, a quality somewhat lacking in Bedford Square, for instance, where both canted bay-fronted and bow-fronted facades appear.

7F Portland Place.

7F Portland Place

Whilst Kemp Town was being built, a series of squares, places and terraces were designed to occupy the space which lay between Royal Crescent and Chichester Terrace. A number of these projects were under construction by 1826. Portland Place was the first, commenced in 1824, one year after Kemp Town was begun. The landowner, a Major Russell, was an acquaintance of Thomas Read Kemp and was no doubt influenced by the magnificence of the Kemp Town project. His project was to be of similar style, but on a smaller scale. The scheme was for a double row of inward facing houses with a large classical villa for the owner sited on axis to the north. The houses were set apart to give the villa an uninterrupted vista to the sea. Charles Busby was the architect and perhaps a clue is given here to the importance of the part he played in the Kemp Town project as a member of the Wilds and Busby partnership. The articulation of one house facade adorned with Corinthian pilasters followed by two houses of plain facade is exactly similar to that used for Lewes Crescent and Sussex Square. Unfortunately the classical villa for Major Russell, its construction well advanced, was completely destroyed by fire in the late summer of 1825. It was not reconstructed but replaced by three houses forming the north end of Portland Place.

7G Eastern Terrace

The whole L-shaped terrace dates from 1828: it is a formal group of individually fine Georgian houses marred only by the removal of the original glazing bars and the addition of second floor balconies. They stand four storeys high with attics and basements, the first two houses (Nos. 1 and 2) and the last two houses (Nos. 8 and 9) have bow fronts. No. 7 has a concave facade and all are stuccoed except for the centre three houses (Nos. 5-7), which are local yellow brick above ground floor. Porches are pillared with Doric columns and with a plain entablature. Their most notable features are fine internal staircases, especially at Nos. 1 and 9. No. 1, once occupied by Sir Albert Sassoon, has almost circular rooms and was claimed to be in its original form the finest house in Brighton.

7H Belgrave Place

Belgrave Place was built by Thomas Cubitt in 1846. It is located on part of the land east of Eastern Terrace which Kemp conveyed to him as payment for building work carried out by Cubitt at Kemp Town and in London. Consisting of seventeen houses, Nos. 1-3 and 13-17 were originally three storeys and a basement, while the rest were four. All of the houses have rusticated stucco ground floors and stucco upper floors and have round headed windows and doorways with semi-

7G Eastern Terrace.

circular fanlights at the ground floor. The house at the top of the Place presents a slightly projecting pediment with title and a date.

7H Belgrave Place.

7J Percival and Clarendon Terraces
Percival and Clarendon Terraces are two fine bow fronted terraces on the seafront. They were built as a speculation from 1845-1850 for William Percival Boxall by Cheeseman and Sons, a local building firm. The land was bought from Cubitt by Boxall and had originally been part of that conveyed to Cubitt by T. R. Kemp in 1828 in return for building work. They are five storeys high with basement, each with three windows in the bow; stuccoed and with a rusticated ground floor. It is possible that the architect was either Cheeseman who designed elsewhere in Brighton or J. T. Knowles the elder, father of Sir James Knowles who took Nos. 3 and 4, since the restrained classical style of the terraces has much in common with his work. The style is more delicate than that of the 1820s. The bow fronts are gently curved, windows have moulded surrounds with delicate cornices finely profiled. The elegant cast iron balconies emphasise the first floor level in a simple and most effective manner.

7J Clarendon Terrace.

7K Kemp Town.

7K Kemp Town

Thomas Read Kemp (1782-1844), born of a wealthy and influential family in Lewes, owned open land east of Royal Crescent which stretched from the Cliff up to Brighton Race Course on the Downs. He was the son of the Member of Parliament for Lewes, one of the Joint Lords of the Manor and later he became a local MP. Kemp was probably inspired by the new Marylebone Estate which came to be known as Regent's Park, being built by John Nash in London. This example, combined with the need to improve his financial situation, led him in 1823 to conceive the idea of building a huge estate in Brighton to attract wealthy middle class inhabitants and visitors to an open site away from the restricted streets of the Old Town.

The development was conceived on a grand scale as a wide square open to the sea, introduced to the seafront by an elegant Crescent and finally flanked by fine terraces. Behind were to be smaller squares and streets for the less wealthy and St. George's Chapel of Ease (8C). A total of 250 houses were planned, but only 106 were built. The remainder were to be in terraces to the rear of the two seafront terraces. Kemp was dominant in the evolution and management of the scheme, and the architects Wilds and Busby were employed to lay out the site and prepare designs for the elevations. Work started in 1823 and the houses sold off as carcasses often with only the facade built, which led to their varied inside arrangement. Most of the facades were completed by 1828 and during the following twenty-five years the carcasses were completed to the owner's taste. They were all built on five storeys with public rooms on the ground and first floors and bedrooms on the floors above. The main kitchen was in the basement and there was a courtyard or light well surrounded on two sides by a lower annexe with a stable and coach house mews beyond. Servants were housed in the basement and on the top floor.

In 1827 Kemp took up residence in the second house to be completed in order to give the development social standing.

Thomas Cubitt, the London builder, became involved when Kemp's finances became strained. Cubitt was well known for his work in Belgravia and throughout London. Kemp's influence waned and more land was passed to Cubitt whose power and involvement increased: he was elected to the Management Committee from where he became the driving force behind the scheme. The single most expensive undertaking was the Esplanade. This was completed by Cubitt in 1835 to the designs of H. E. Kendall Jnr., Thomas Kemp's architect, and it involved the landscaping of the adjacent beach, the building of recreational and management facilities and connection to the Crescent via a tunnel.

By overseeing the works Cubitt could ensure the scheme's completion and affirm his stamp of quality. The houses were normally of brick, stuccoed to resemble stone, with brick and stone porches and Portland Stone "Trafalgar" balconies. The overall effect was a project of unusual spaciousness, three storeys with attics relying on scale and proportion rather than rich elaborate architectural treatment to achieve it. Only one house in three has Corinthian pilasters and these are on plain facades.

The speculation ruined Kemp, but his concept has an endearing urban character and is still well loved by all those who live there today.

7L Chichester Place Mews.

7L Chichester Place Mews

Behind Chichester Terrace is a row of three-storey houses arranged around a quiet central court. They are a modern addition to Kemp Town designed by Mark Hills, of APP (Brighton) on behalf of the Hatley group of companies. They are flanked to the south by the rear of Thomas Cubitt's grand terrace and to the east by the mews buildings which were built as coachhouses and stabling. The development seeks to use modern construction techniques to provide houses which reflect the lifestyles of today's clients much as the Georgian designs did in the 1820s.

This scheme is a success largely because the designer has chosen not simply to ape the detail and motifs of the late Regency but to abstract their forms and thereby inject fresh ideas and imagination into the work.

7M Chichester Terrace.

7M Chichester Terrace

The last part of the Kemp Town development to be completed was probably Chichester Terrace, built in the 1850s. For many years it stood with only Chichester House at its west end and three houses at its east end. In August 1830 Cubitt acquired eleven properties here but in that decade built only No. 11, his "Fireproof" house, which tested his theories on fireproof construction. The rest of the terrace had much of the design detail omitted and only No. 1 exhibits the typical Corinthian pilastered facade of Wilds and Busby. All have cast iron balustrading to balconies with hoods over porches with fluted Doric columns. The original design, however, was to match the facade of Arundel Terrace, a more elaborate composition.

7N Lewes Crescent

Lewes Crescent is 200 feet wider than the Royal Crescent at Bath and has fourteen houses on each side. Thomas Cubitt, who rapidly became a major landowner here, sold No. 1 Lewes Crescent to the Duke of Devonshire, who also owned No. 14 Chichester Terrace. The similarity of the plan to some of his London houses, notably the oval stair top lit by a skylight, leads one to assume that the design was by Cubitt. Cubitt

7N Lewes Crescent.

7N Lewes Crescent.

took No. 13 as his own residence. The facade of every third house has Corinthian pilasters from the first floor to the second and plain pilasters from cornice to parapet. All houses have cast iron balustrades to balconies and a string course above the windows on the first floor. The slope of the site is taken up by stepping each ensemble of three houses with common floor and cornice levels.

7P The original concept.

7P Sussex Square

Sussex Square was designed as the focus of Kemp's great scheme. A square of 50 houses, again inspired by Nash's terraces off Regents Park, with elevations which unfortunately cannot be read as a whole because of the scale of the square. Thomas Kemp was quick to move into No. 22 in 1827, almost alone in the skeletal composition, from where he organised many parties to encourage prospective owners. Thomas Cubitt took possession of his five houses here, Nos. 7-10, in December 1826, to which he added adequate stabling, later called Arundel Mews.

7Q Arundel Terrace

Consisting of thirty-nine bays of symmetrical composition, Arundel Terrace shows the direction that Wilds and Busby wanted to continue. It was the first portion of Kemp Town to be completed by 1828 and the only one designed and built as a whole. Symmetrical in layout it has a centrepiece of five houses. Of these the central house has completely detached Corinthian columns and a projecting entablature supporting a balcony. The two houses on either side of the centre have attached Corinthian columns between pillars setting back and then setting forward whilst on each side of this columnated quintet are three plain houses. The end houses, Nos. 1 and 13, are again set forward with attached Corinthian columns. Sadly some of the houses' original fronts have been marred by the addition of second floor balconies and some cutting of cornices. The end of Arundel Terrace signifies the eastern boundary of Georgian Brighton.

7Q Arundel Terrace.

7R Maison Francaise De Retraite Et De Convalescence

The French Convalescent Home, glibly dismissed as a "dreary institution" by Pevsner is another interesting example of the work of Clayton and Black, architects for the King and Queen public house (see 3P) and the building now used by "The Leeds Permanent Building Society" (see 5L).

It was built in 1898 to serve as a convalescent home for patients from the French Hospital in London's Shaftesbury Avenue. While the French Renaisance style might seem out of place on Brighton's seafront; it was presumably felt to be appropriate by its inmates.

7R Maison Francaise.

7S Marine Gate

This residential block at the very edge of Brighton was designed by the firm of Wimperis, Simpson and Guthrie. Built between 1937 and 1939 these flats are a good example of quality 'thirties' apartments which compare favourably with those in Embassy Court (see 9J), a contemporary building on the western seafront. The plan strove to allow every flat a view of the sea and some an additional view of the downland behind. Originally comprising 120 flats with internal access to a communal garage and a restaurant, the latter was subsequently removed to provide more residential accommodation.

The flats vary in size from one to four bedrooms with more than adequate bathroom facilities expressed on the facade with circular windows. Each flat has a balcony and fitted furniture to add to the indisputable spaciousness and elegant proportions. The building is steel framed, allowing the internal walls to be non-loadbearing and allowing future flexibility. Set back from the road the U shaped block has a well conceived road access to the entrance with landscaping between it and Marine Drive; it was one of the first blocks to anticipate the demise of short leased properties. Residents are shareholders in the company owning the head lease.

7S Marine Gate.

8 KEMP TOWN, ST. JAMES'S & QUEEN'S PARK

The area lying behind the eastern seafront has been built up since the beginning of the 19th century on land which had previously formed part of Brighton's common field system. The land lying between Eastern Road and Marine Parade was developed during the early Victorian period in the wake of the fashionable seafront developments which appeared during the first decades of the century. The Carlton Hill area was built up during the early 19th century as mean terraced houses which quickly developed into slums and was cleared and redeveloped with local authority flats soon after the 2nd World War. Queen's Park is a late Victorian and Edwardian suburb, all red bricks and clay tiles. Below Queen's Park the Freshfield Industrial Estate occupies the site of the former Kemp Town Railway station. To the east is Whitehawk, a large and rather bleak estate of low density local authority housing built originally between the wars to rehouse people from the worst areas of Carlton Hill. Beyond it is the Racecourse and the Downs.

8A Kemp Town Mews

The fine houses which grew up along Brighton's seafront during the early years of the 19th century were planned with open fields behind them. But the lifestyle which they promised depended on a network of service and support and soon the fields were eaten up by a grid of streets corresponding to the paulpieces of the East Laine. Here were to be found the less fashionable lodging houses, the shops, the neat cottages of tradesmen and domestic servants, the workshops and the stables. The grand seafront terraces backed on to their own mews where horses, carriages and coachmen could be lodged. Good examples of such mews can still be seen behind Eastern Terrace, Chichester Terrace and Sussex Square. The mews behind Chichester Terrace reveal a cheerful collection of brick and flint buildings, some retaining a number of original stable features, and are used mainly as private residences.

8A Sussex Mews.

8B The Bombay Bar
Paston Place

The present billiard room of the Hanbury Arms was originally built in 1892 as a mausoleum for Sir Albert Sassoon, a wealthy merchant with business interests in India. The Sassoons lived at 1 Eastern Terrace on the sea-front and the mausoleum occupied a corner of their back garden. It was built in an oriental style which reflected both the family's origins and the influences of the Royal Pavilion. The mausoleum was contained within a cube of masonry under a circular tent-shaped copper dome. It was finished in white stucco and decorated with marbles and arabesques. Sir Albert was buried there in 1896 and joined by his son Edward in 1912. In 1933 the bodies were transferred to another resting place and the mausoleum was incorporated into the neighbouring public house.

8C St. George the Martyr
St. Georges' Road

The Wilds-Busby partnership built four of Brighton's surviving churches, two of them for Thomas Read Kemp, the developer of Kemp Town. The first was a chapel in Ship Street built in 1817 by Amon Wilds to house Kemp's own sect. The sect was somewhat unorthodox and its chapel was unconventional. The east facing front was formed by a Doric tetrastyle portico and the interior was lit by a glass roof lantern. Kemp abandoned the sect in 1822 and in 1825 the Ship Street Chapel was taken over by the Church of England and renamed as the Church of the Holy Trinity. At this time the portico was removed and replaced by a sever 5 bay front with a plain pediment. In 1867 the church was substantially rebuilt behind a Gothic front when Duke Street was widened, and is of little interest today. In 1820 Amon Henry Wilds built the Unitarian Chapel in New Road (see 1F) and again used a Doric tetrastyle portico. A third commission came again from Kemp who had by now returned to the Church of England. In 1824 he obtained the necessary Act of Parliament to construct a church to serve the new suburb of Kemp Town and appointed Charles Busby as his architect. This was no act of charity: churches were a good investment and the owner could expect a steady income from pew rents. The new church was opened in 1825, having cost £11,000 to build. It is one of Busby's most successful buildings and one of Brighton's few surviving Georgian churches. The main body of the church is a plain box of yellow brick with two tiers of windows under a heavy cornice. The west front has a pair of ionic columns recessed between square pilasters on either side of the entrance and is topped by an attractive square tower and

8C St. George The Martyr.

cupola. The church was a favourite of Queen Adelaide and, such was its popularity, a gallery or "sky parlour" was added after 1830 to provide extra seats. At this time Busby's interiors were destroyed and the original Ionic pilasters were replaced by cast iron columns decorated with acanthus capitals. Kemp later sold the church to the Peel family who eventually sold it to the congregation. Further alterations were carried out in 1890. In 1962 the church was threatened with demolition, but the trustees resisted and later carried out extensive renovations.

8D St. John the Baptist
Bristol Road
This early catholic church was built in 1835 by William Hallet with support from Mrs. Fitzherbert, the sometime wife of the Prince Regent. The main front has a pediment raised on two Corinthian columns in antis. The interior contains fine sculpture by John Edward Carew, including a monument to Mrs. Fitzherbert who is buried in the crypt. Substantial alterations were carried out during the 1870s and 1880s and this was the first catholic church in the country to receive electric lighting. In 1937 H. S. Goodhart Rendell supervised extensive restoration work.

8E Old Stables
Wyndham Street
This attractive Victorian brick-built stable building has a large lancet arch flanked on both sides by a trio of smaller lancets with decorative dressing of black and white stone. A plaque on the central gable dates the building at 1866.

8F St. Mary the Virgin
St. James's Street
This church was designed by Sir William Emerson and built in 1877. Emerson worked in India where he is remembered for the Victoria Monument in Calcutta and for his collaboration with Lutyens, and this is his only known work in this country. The exterior is of red brick in an Early English style. The stained glass is by Clayton and Bell.

8G St. Mary's Hall
Eastern Road
The school was founded in 1836 by the Rev. H. Elliot and was built on land donated by the Marquis of Bath with money raised by public subscription. The main building was designed by George Basevi, who is better known as the architect of the Fitzwilliam Museum in Cambridge, and is an imposing stuccoed block in a severe symmetrical Tudor style sitting on a raised platform. A chapel was added during the 1840s. Later the school acquired an adjoining house on Eastern Road, but this suffered bomb damage during the war and was later rebuilt in 1951 with typical post-war detailing. Recently a new swimming pool and sixth from block have been built by John Schwerdt and partners of Lewes.

8H The Royal Sussex County Hospital
Eastern Road
The land for the new hospital was donated by Thomas Read Kemp and money came from private benefactors, among them Lord Egremont. The selection of the architect was surrounded by some controversy. Charles Busby who was closely associated with Kemp clearly expected the commission, but it went

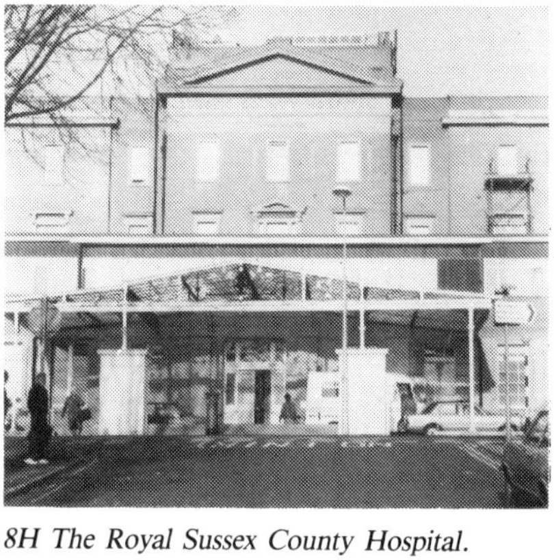

8H The Royal Sussex County Hospital.

to Charles Barry through the intervention of Edward Everard, who was secretary of the trustees and was Barry's client for St. Andrew's Church in Waterloo Street (see ION). Barry had already pipped the Wilds Busby partnership in the 1824 competition to design St. Peter's Church in the Steine (see 3L), and now Busby was moved to write a protest letter to the Brighton Herald. The hospital was in fact designed by Barry, and finally opened in 1828. Since then it has been much altered and extended. The Victoria Wing was added in 1837 to designs by William Hallet (see 8D). Three years later Herbert Williams designed the Adelaide Wing to the east, and in 1856 the Marquis of Bristol donated a chapel. Later 19th century additions were by E. E. Scott while in the 1920s new work was designed by F. T. Cawthorn. The site is now dominated by the tall ward block which was during the early 1970s designed by the Health Authority's own architects.

8J Brighton College
Eastern Road

This boys' public school was founded by Henry Michell Wagner in order "to provide a thoroughly liberal and practical education in conformity with the principles of the established church". The architect, G. G. Scott, was selected after a competition and the foundation stone was laid in 1848. The main building is of knapped flint with stone dressings in a "joyless" sub-gothic style. Scott also designed the School House (1854) and the Chapel (1859). The south range with the entrance archway was designed in 1886 by Sir Thomas Jackson, an old boy of the school, who went on to design a number of additions during the next 40 years. F. T. Cawthorn designed the School Hall in 1913 and more recent additions have been added by Clayton and Black, APP and the Miller Bourne Partnership.

8K American Express — "Amex House"
Edward Street

Amex House dominates the sweep of Carlton Hill. Built in 1977 to designs by Gollins Melvin and Ward it makes a much more successful addition to Edward Street than its contemporary neighbours. The horizontality of the main elevations fails to disguise the building's bulk, but the architects avoided adding another tower block to Brighton's skyline. Indeed the combination of white GRP panels, used here for the first time in this country and still impressively clean, and blue tinted glass seems to be an appropriate one for a contemporary Brighton building. Amex House is the European Headquarters of American Express.

8L Public Buildings in Edward Street

Edward Street first appears on Marchant's map of 1808 and follows the line of the old "leakway" which ran between Hilly Laine and Little Laine. Although if formed a main route to the eastern parts of the town it remained narrow and congested until 1928 when many old properties were demolished to permit widening to take place. Since then a number of public buildings, among them new Law Courts and Police Station, have appeared in graceless fashion along the northern side of the street, while the southern side has been allowed to slide towards dereliction. Edward Street today lends credence to the notion that modern planning has contributed little to Brighton, and that modern architecture has failed to provide civic monuments of quality.

8M Queen's Park as originally conceived by Barry.

8M Queen's Park — The Pepperpot

William Attree, a successful solicitor and a leading figure in Brighton society, was inspired by Regent's Park in London to develop an exclusive estate of villas around a park. He acquired land to the north of Eastern Road and in 1825 appointed Charles Barry to be his architect. The venture was not a success and only one villa, that occupied by Attree himself, was completed to Barry's design. The Attree Villa was obliterated in 1971 and all that remains of Barry's work is the pepperpot tower which was built to house the estate's pump and water tank and which today serves as a most elegant public lavatory. The archway at the head of Egremont Place is another remnant of Attree's scheme, but it cannot be linked with Barry. The house plots around the park were developed individually, but the park remained and in 1890 the Brighton Race Stands Trustees purchased all 7 hectares for £13,500 and presented them as a gift to the town. Today the park serves as a very attractive focal point to a largely Edwardian suburb.

8M The Attree Villa.

8N The German Spa and Nursery School Park Hill

The German Spa was opened in the southern corner of Queen's Park in 1825 by Dr. F. A. A. Struve of Dresden. Struve had developed methods to manufacture artificial spa waters to resemble the natural waters found in places like Marienbad, and had already opened similar spas in Dresden, Leipzig and Berlin. The spa was an immediate success and during the 1830s people flocked to take the waters each morning between 8.00 a.m. and 10.00 a.m. The pump room was housed behind an

8N The Spa in its heyday.

elegant Ionic colonnade, the ruins of which still exist. The spa seems to have closed sometime towards the end of the 1850s and for many years was occupied by a firm of mineral water manufacturers which went under the name of Hooper Struve Ltd. Hooper Struve closed in 1962 and the buildings fell into ruin. Plans to open a casino met with vigorous opposition from local residents and finally the site was used to build a new nursery school. The school was designed by the East Sussex County Architects to fit with the ruins of the spa and was one of the most attractive modern buildings in Brighton until it was destroyed by fire in 1985. Reconstruction is now underway.

8N The ruins of the German Spa.

8P St. Luke's School and Pool
St. Luke's Terrace

St. Luke's School was built in 1903 to serve the growing community which had developed around Queen's Park. It was designed by Thomas Simpson of Brighton and offers today a very well preserved example of school building from the turn of the century. The monumental scale of the buildings is partly the result of the height of the ceilings which were raised to admit light and air into the classrooms. The style is vaguely Queen Anne and there is a profusion of rich decoration in the detailing. The school was provided with its own swimming pool which was lit by a magnificent glazed roof. In 1986 the pool was extensively modernised when the old marine boiler was replaced after 80 years of service and the glass roof was hidden by an energy saving suspended ceiling.

8P St. Luke's School.

8Q Trinity Church
Carlton Hill

Formerly known as St. John the Evangelist, this church was built by George Cheesman in 1838 for Henry Michell Wagner. The severe classical front faces south and has a blank centre flanked by giant Doric pilasters with doors located in the side bays under small pediments. The altar is in the east and the visitor performs a right-turn upon entering. The interior has an intimate scale produced partly by the deep gallery which is supported on cast iron Doric columns. This is quite unlike the untutored gothic of Cheesman's exactly contemporary St. John-Sub-Castro in Lewes. The church is used by the Greek community and a modern altar screen has been installed.

9 THE WESTERN SEAFRONT

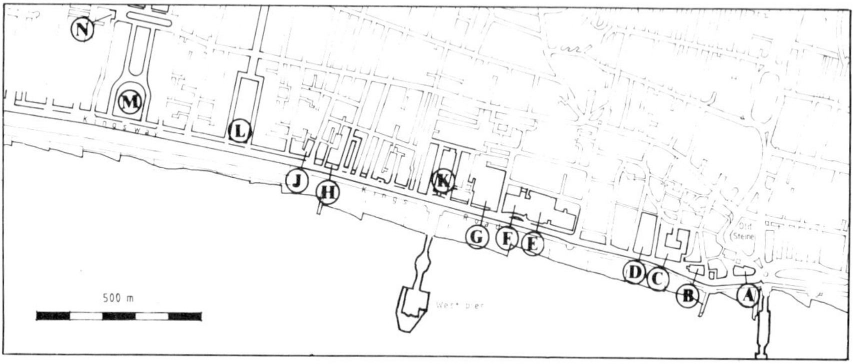

Until the late 17th century when coastal erosion removed it, the southern boundary of the old town was defined by the market place. It formed the main east to west thoroughfare along the seafront. After its destruction by erosion, traffic could no longer traverse along the cliffs between West and East Street and was compelled to turn up Middle Street, proceed along Middle Street Lane into South Street and then down West Street. This remained throughout the eighteenth century. King Street was constructed in 1822 as a replacement, at least in part, of South Street. It ran between Middle Street and West Street and its opening commemorated the ascension of George IV. The new road, the construction of which was supervised by A. H. Wilds, did not fully reinstate a direct East-West route along the cliff and it was not until 1829, after the building of the sea wall in 1825-27, that the through route was completed by the Grand Junction Road. Five years later, in 1834, the Esplanade was constructed between Artillery Place (where the Grand Hotel now stands) and Brunswick Terrace, with supervision again by A. H. Wilds.

The expansion of Brighton into Hove, in the 1820s and 1830s, saw the development of the Brunswick Estate and Adelaide Crescent but it is difficult to discern visually exactly where the town boundary lies. The difference in style and layout is more clearly pronounced however just to the west of Adelaide Crescent by the wider avenues, roads and lawns of Hove. Kingsway was named after Edward VII, whose statue stands astride the town's boundary.

9A The Royal Albion Hotel

Until the completion of the Bedford Hotel by Thomas Cooper in 1829, the Royal Albion and the somewhat earlier Royal York were the most exclusive hotels in town. Designed by A. H. Wilds and opened in 1829 the Royal Albion was built partly on the site of the residence of Doctor Russell, the renowned medical practitioner who "invented the sea" and who lived there from 1752 until his death in 1759. After Russell House was demolished in the 1820s a gap was created which allowed an open view to the sea on the southern side of the Steine. It was suggested at the time that the Town Commissioners should acquire the site for the agreed sum of £6,000 as permanent open space offering a vista from the Steine to the English Channel, but delays prevented this from taking place and the Royal Albion Hotel was built on the site. Whether the resulting containment of the Steine is preferable is a matter for conjecture.

9A The Royal Albion Hotel.

The original building, on the eastern section of the site, is a symmetrical composition, rectangular and cubic shaped, and was initially free standing. Its facade is of rusticated stucco at ground floor, with first and second floors articulated with Corinthian pilasters and attached Corinthian columns with reciprocal break front entablature emphasising the centrality of the composition. One of A. H. Wilds' trademarks appears on the third floor of the four storey structure where semi-circular shell ornamentation is used above the windows. This device was employed by Wilds in Oriental Place (see 10H). The mansard roof is partly concealed behind the parapet. The hotel was so successful that shortly after completion the building was extended and a four storey block attached to it parallel to the sea-front and on the west side. The intercolumnation is wider and the order is now Tuscan for pilasters with central recessed Ionic attached columns. Clearly the fourth floor and ungainly mansard roof were of a much later date than the ground floor extension to the east.

9B Queen's Hotel

The site was originally occupied by an inn called the Dolphin which was demolished in 1846. Next door were the famous vapour baths run by Sheikh Mahomed who had been Shampooing Surgeon to King George IV. The baths were later converted in 1869 into Markwells Hotel which was eventually absorbed into the Queens Hotel.

9D The Old Ship Hotel.

9C The Ramada Renaissance Hotel

This new hotel is part of a major redevelopment of the land between Brighton Town Hall and Kings Road which is the result of partnership between Speyhawk Land and Estates, the developers, and Brighton Borough Council, the owners of the freehold of the site. The architects are Michael Lyell and Associates of London. The development consists of five main elements: a five star hotel, new civic offices, a suite of lettable offices, a new civic square and a basement car park. The hotel will be operated by Ramada International Ltd. as part of its Renaissance chain. It is planned around a central landscaped atrium which is located at first floor level. There are 211 air-conditioned bedrooms of which only a quarter have views of the sea while a large proportion are perversely oriented towards the atrium. The rear of the hotel faces into the new civic square which is formed by the Town Hall (see 2C) and the new office block and which will be surrounded at ground floor level by shops. The main elevation forms a bland wall of pre-cast concrete cladding relieved by glazed bay windows, a polite but uninspired addition to the seafront. Completion is expected in mid 1987.

9D The Old Ship Hotel

The oldest licensed house in Brighton, The Old Ship was certainly in existence in the early 1600s and is probably Elizabethan, although there is no information to suggest the actual date of the original building. Enlarged in the 1750s by the proprietor, William Hicks, who built the basis of what became the Assembly Rooms to counteract the rivalry of the Castle Tavern. A decade later, it was further extended by his grandson John Hicks who engaged William Golden to build the Assembly Rooms, comprising a card room, a coffee room and a ballroom. Only the card room, with its shallow barrel vaulted ceiling, remains in some semblance of the original Adam-styled decorations.

Further extensions have been added since that date, including the western corner on Ship Street, which was added in 1838, the acquisition of two houses on East Cliff in the 1890s, the redevelopment of the garage and stable area in 1928, the further acquisition of yet more houses in Ship Street in 1937 and finally, and more recently, the East Wing on the corner of Black Lion Street, which was added in 1963-64.

9E The Brighton Conference Centre Kings Road

The Brighton Conference Centre was designed by Russell Diplock and Associates and opened in 1977. It is a part of the massive redevelopment of the site bounded in the north by Western Road, in the east by the rear of West Street and in the south by the seafront, which includes the Kingswest entertainment complex and Churchill Square (see 10B). The main conference hall at first floor level is 40 metres by 47 metres and is spanned by 10 warren trusses. It has a maximum seating capacity of 5,000, half of it accommodated on balconies on three sides, and half in the form of movable seating on the flat floor. Although it has been designed principally as a conference centre, the main hall can also accommodate sporting events, banquets or even ice spectaculars. Around the main hall is grouped the service and ancillary accommodation with a restaurant and bars, a secondary hall and an exhibition space. The main entrance foyer is off Kings Road and leads up to a smaller foyer which serves the two halls and connects to a second entrance on the land side. The centre has proved to be a great success and its flexibility has been thoroughly tested. There can be no doubt that it represents the sort of investment in new facilities which Brighton desperately needs. What a pity that, along with its neighbour the Kingswest Building, it could not have been handled architecturally with more wit and with less disregard for the panorama of Kings Road!

9E Brighton Conference Centre.

9F The Grand Hotel

When it was opened in 1864 the Grand Hotel was the largest hotel in Brighton. Designed by the architect J. H. Whichcord, it was in a free Italianate cum French Second Empire style as used by Cuthbert Brodrick for the Grand Hotel Scarborough and by Sir James Knowles at the Grosvenor in London Victoria. The hotel occupies the site on which stood Artillery Place, a Regency Crescent that incorporated the old West Battery House and ammunition ground, all of which was destroyed when the Grand was built. The style of the building was criticised at the time for being inappropriate to the realities of the English climate since it had bronzed and gilded balconies, elaborate ornamentation and roof pavilions. It was, however, innovative in a number of ways, not least its height which rises eight storeys and is emphasised by corner towers.

9F The Grand Hotel.

Accommodating 150 bedrooms, the hotel was one of the first to have lift and electrical installations and it was said to boast 30 miles of flooring, 23,500 cubic feet of timber and 6 miles of gas piping. The building was severely damaged in October 1984 when a bomb exploded on one of the upper floors, but fortunately it has been saved by restoration and refurbishment amounting to several million pounds. Externally the west side annex has now been increased in height to match the east side. A glazed sun lounge in a Victorian style has been added at ground floor.

9G The Metropole Hotel

In its original form this was in the unmistakable style of Alfred Waterhouse, designer of town halls at Manchester and Hove. This high Victorian hotel with its bright red brick and terracotta facade was built in 1888-90 at a cost of £57,000. It was as great a departure from the earlier Victorian hotels like the Norfolk and the Grand as they in their time were from the hotels of Wilds and Busby. Although thought by some to be the ugliest building in town, the Metropole had the most extensive facilities of any hotel in Brighton or indeed outside London with

9H The Norfolk Hotel.

Turkish, Russian and Vapour baths, and a suite of conference rooms. Patronised by a number of famous names, including Winston Churchill and John F. Kennedy, it was used as a base during the war for the Royal Australian and the Royal New Zealand Air Forces. Subsequent to threats of demolition the building was extensively modernised and enlarged in 1961 by R. Seifert and Partners. Two additional storeys were added which sadly necessitated the removal of Waterhouse's central copper spire and turrets from the original roofline. The additional accommodation which resulted from this work included 192 new bedrooms, 50 new flats, and a rooftop restaurant. In addition nine new conference and exhibition halls and a 300 foot tower, Sussex Heights, were built on the northern part of the site at the same time.

9G The Metropole Hotel.

9H The Norfolk Hotel

Reminiscent of the Grand Hotel and also of E. M. Barry's London hotels, the Norfolk Hotel replaced the Norfolk Arms which had existed on the site since 1824. Designed by Horatio Goultry and completed in 1865 it has a stucco facade, cast iron balconies and arched windows with segmental architraves and keystones. The mansard roof is in three separate sections with wrought iron cresting.

9J Embassy Court

Embassy Court, a good example of the early Modern Movement work in England, and one of the very few in the Sussex area, was designed by Wells Coates with D. Pleydell-Bouverie in the mid 1930s and constructed in 1936. Some elements within the design are reminiscent of the work of Erich Mendelsohn. Wells Coates visited several of Mendelsohn's buildings whilst in Germany in 1931-32.

Comprising 69 flats on twelve floors, there are seven flats per floor on the first to eighth floors and variations on the ground and ninth and tenth floors, which include the first penthouse suites built in England. The plan is devised with setbacks from the continuous concrete spandrels which form balconies and allow living rooms a view of the sea. Where glazing is forward on the spandrel sun rooms are provided with subtly curved windows which have a nice vertical rhythm. This does much to alleviate the horizontal layers of concrete spandrels and windows, particularly on the longer elevation and perspective to Western Street. A similar emphasis of the cantilevered access decks on the rear elevation is punctuated by the projecting lift and service core and the diagonals of the external stairs. Although the window levels were designed to relate to the adjoining four and five storey late Georgian terrace houses, the sheer height of the building is only partly mitigated by the

9J Embassy Court.

9K Regency Square.

setbacks on 9th and 10th floors.

The contextualist comment has been that the building could have made a more sympathetic response to its surroundings had the setback occurred after the fifth floor. Embassy Court suffered major constructional and maintenance problems shortly after completion, but is was in some respects quite innovative. All electric servicing was provided and unlimited hot water was supplied by an electric thermo storage system housed in the basement. Space heating was from ceiling panels supplemented by specially designed electric fires.

The building remains today well maintained and much as it was when first completed in the mid 1930s, except for the sun rooms, many of which have been incorporated into living spaces within the flats. There was a plan to redevelop much of the seafront in a similar style.

9K Regency Square

Laid out by the landowner Joshua Flesher Hanson in 1818 the site had been known until then as Belle Vue Field and had been used for fairs, shows and military reviews. The field probably derived its name from Belle Vue House owned by Count de St. Antonio. No longer in existence, the house was located to the west of the site. The scheme for development consisted initially of enclosing the central garden and dividing the site into 70 plots which were then let by Hanson with building options. The plots were taken quickly and developed by builders who were compelled by deed of covenant to conform to a specific design for the facades. The architects are believed to have been Amon Wilds in partnership with his son Amon Henry Wilds, although there is no evidence to substantiate this. Charles Busby was almost certainly not involved in the scheme since the buildings appear to lack his distinctive flair. Designed in the tradition of the terrace town house which had been established by Henry Holland in Hans town and Sloane Street in London and by Robert Adam, there were bow fronts on the ground and first floors, some of them with canopies over, along with classical entrance porches. Originally the covenant was quite specific about materials to be used externally. The ground and first floors were required to be faced with stucco and upper floors were to be finished with yellow bricks and stone dressings. By 1828 the majority of the square was complete. Nos. 47-50 are of a design which indicate a later date. No. 1, now St. Albans also of a later date, was designed by A. H. Wilds and is historically the most interesting house in the square. Named after its occupier in the 1830s, the Duchess of St. Albans, who was married first to Thomas Coutts the banker and then to the Duke of Albans, it had attached to it a riding school which was claimed to be the largest interior space in England, second in size only to Westminster Abbey. This was demolished after the second world war and the site used for the car park to the Bedford Hotel.

9L Brunswick Square and Terrace

The Brunswick Estate was built very much on the same basis as St. James or Bloomsbury in London. Its boundaries defined by Lansdowne Place and Waterloo Street, Upper Western Road and the seafront, it occupies the south eastern section of what was Wick Farm. In contrast with many London estates the landowner was not an aristocrat, but a clergyman, the Reverend Thomas Scutt, who did not live on the estate. Evidence suggests that although the Wilds and Busby partnership were the architects, Charles Busby was responsible for the design and may well have initiated the idea of the scheme. A complete unit of development was envisaged, including a square, secondary streets, a market and baths. A church was added later, but was not part of the estate. The idea of living in an elegant terrace house which was part of a large neo-classic palace style composition was first employed at Bath and then at Regents Park. Like Kemp Town and Regents Park in London the houses were five storeys with rear annexes around internal courtyards and mews buildings beyond, in which coaches and horses were kept.

The name of the estate was derived from the contemporary Royal House. Work began on the eastern section of Brunswick Terrace in 1824. This section was finished in 1828, but many houses in the terrace were occupied before that date. Both the eastern and western halves of the terrace were almost entirely let as furnished houses for the season because of their prominent position by the sea, whilst the square was sold as private houses. The terraces were given symmetrical facades modelled on Nash's terraces in Regents Park. They have central porticos embracing three houses and end pavilions of one house. The porticos and end pavilions have attached giant Corinthian columns between end Corinthian pillars and individual acanthus leaved cast iron balconies at first floor, whilst the houses between have Corinthian pilasters and continuous balconies.

The square was started in 1825 and with a few exceptions was complete by 1828. An articulation of ensembles of Ionic columned and Tuscan pilastered houses with individual balconies between columns of continuous balconies across the single facade, the Square is composed of groups of four houses with

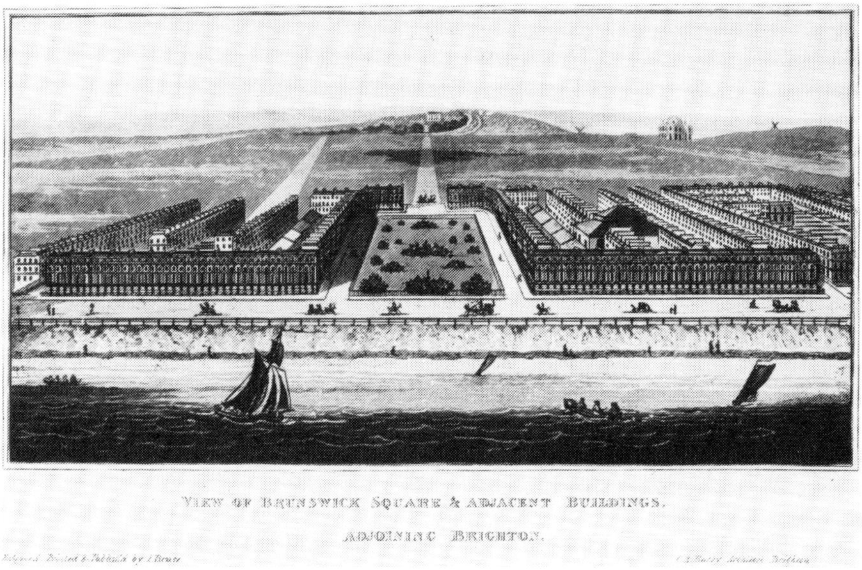

9L Brunswick Square.

unbroken cornice lines and the stepping of facades to respond to the sloping site occurs between each quartet. The houses with Ionic columns have recessed porches with Doric columns favoured by Charles Busby who hated "the Roman decadence of Robert Adam". The facade system is interrupted by slightly later houses which are narrower than the adjoining houses and have a more pronounced bow on the front facade. They occupy spaces which were initially intended to be left as access ways to the mews at the rear of the houses. The northern sides of the square are later and less embellished, but the north end and the eight houses of Brunswick Place (below Western Road) pick up the giant pilasters of the terrace again.

Built as domestic units, the houses of Brunswick Square and Terrace are similar in plan to Lewes Crescent. With domestic offices in the basement, a dining room and hall on the ground floor and a double drawing room on the first floor, the second floor contained bedrooms and the third floor servants' quarters. In 1830 the residents of the Brunswick Estate obtained an Act of Parliament which allowed them to administer their own affairs through a committee called the Brunswick Commissioners. The Act still applies today and the Brunswick Commissioners are now incorporated in the Hove Corporation.

The Brunswick Estate was designed to be a self-contained unit and service buildings were erected at the same time. These included a market, which became a riding school and is now part of the Old Market Arts Centre, and supporting streets such as Waterloo Street, Upper and Lower Market Streets as well as Brunswick Streets, East and West. There was a small town hall and jail. Besides the market, a hotel was created at 42 Brunswick Terrace called the Brunswick Hotel and now known as the Alexander Hotel.

9M Adelaide Crescent and Palmeira Square

The land on which Adelaide Crescent and Palmeira Square now stands, like Brunswick Town, was owned throughout the eighteenth century by the Scutt family. It constituted part of Wick Farm which extended both to the south and to the north of Western Road. When Brunswick Town was built, the brick yard which had occupied the site was moved into what is now the south west corner of Adelaide Crescent (the boundary of Wick Farm) whilst the rest of the farm consisted of open fields. The only buildings on site were

9L Brunswick Terrace.

Long Barn Cottage and the Wick Inn, which occupies the same position but has been rebuilt. In 1825 Thomas Scutt contracted to sell the whole of the remaining part of his land, including that to the south of Western Road, to Thomas Read Kemp, whose own land adjoined Wick Farm on the east. Apparently Kemp intended to erect on some portion of this land another development of houses similar to that which he was building on the eastern side of Brighton. The project was never realised due to financial problems in Kemp Town and the land was sold eventually to Isaac Lyon Goldsmid in 1830. The son of a bullion broker, he was later made Baron de Goldsmid e da Palmeira for his services to the Queen of Portugal. Work was commenced on Adelaide Crescent in 1830 to the design of Decimus Burton, then aged about 30, who had worked with Nash at Regents Park and six years earlier had designed the Athenaeum Club — Pall Mall. The scheme prepared by Burton was a grand crescent with extended ends treated in each case as a pedimented centralised composition of three houses facing the sea. The north south slope of the site was levelled by raising the crescent and landscaping above the seafront road and approaching the crescent, set on a large 2 metre high balustraded base, by means of symmetrically placed ramps and stairs within heavily rusticated rendered retaining walls. The Crescent was named Queen Adelaide Crescent, which is the full and correct name, with the permission of King William IV.

The first houses to be built were Numbers 1-8 to Decimus Burton's original design and were in the south east corner, with three of the houses facing the sea (formerly Adelaide Terrace) and the remaining five houses forming the first segment of Adelaide Crescent. The houses were complete and all occupied by 1834. They possess a nicety of scale effected by keeping the ground floor only slightly above pavement level and setting the third floor windows between Italianate brackets supporting the cornice and balustrated parapet. During the next sixteen years no further work was carried out. By 1850 the Baron had decided to complete the Crescent, but not as a complete segment of a circle as originally intended. He wished to add Palmeira Square to the north as an extension to the scheme. The rest of the crescent, that is to say Numbers 9-19 on the east side and the whole of the west side, was completed by 1860. The east side was built in a simplified form of the original Burton facades. The level of roofs is stepped, rather than continuous and unbroken as shown in the original design. The houses on the west side are repetitive in design with barely any architectural decoration.

By 1851 plans were being drawn up for Palmeira Square by an architect whose name is not recorded. Since 1832, the site had been occupied by the ruins of the Anthaeum which was to have been the largest conservatory in the world but for a number of disastrous events. The originator of the conservatory was the botanist Henry Phillips and the architect was A. H. Wilds, although he was probably not the designer. The structure was a huge 160 ft. diameter dome of cast iron and glass supported by cast iron ribs and a central column. An argument arose whilst the dome was being constructed as to the necessity of the central support which resulted in the resignation of both the architect and the engineer. Without their supervision the work continued and on 29th August 1833 the building was completed and the contractor, without waiting for instructions, removed all of the scaffolding and the temporary support for the dome. The following day the building suffered structural failure and collapsed. The only occupant, the head gardner, was saved by a warning crack and ran for his life. The debris remained until 1855 when it was cleared to make way for Palmeira Square. Unlike Adelaide Crescent where in its later stages there is evidence of a transition from Georgian to Italianate, Palmeira Square is executed in a Victorian Italianate style, both sides being symmetrical with stucco elevations and central pediments. The first houses to be built were on the west and although the square was completed by 1870, it was not until 1874 that the last house was sold and the whole square occupied.

9N St. John the Baptist, Hove

Isaac Goldsmid's intention to develop the whole of the Wick Farm land purchased in 1830 meant that the completion of Adelaide Crescent and Palmeira Square formed only part of the overall development envisaged. It became obvious that the estate would need a church of its own to accommodate the new residents of the estate. As a result, Baron Goldsmid with the Brunswick Commissioners and the clergy, financed the building of St. John's Church. The architects were W. G. and E. Habershon. The foundation stone was laid in 1852 and the church was consecrated in 1854 by Dr. Gilbert, Bishop of Chichester.

9M Adelaide Crescent.

10 WESTERN ROAD

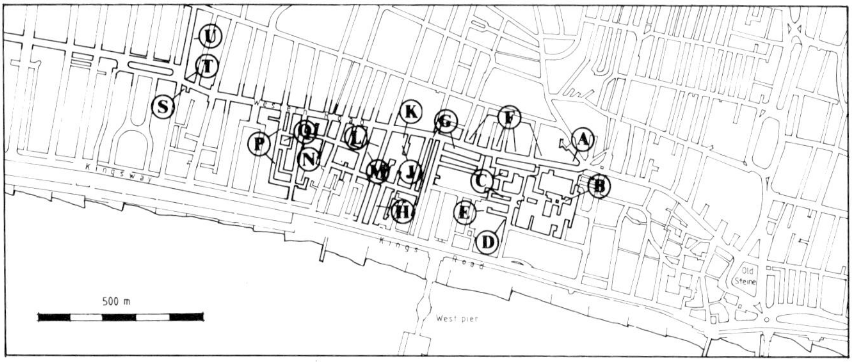

Until the beginning of the 19th century Western Road, named after the Western family of Preston Manor, was little more than a track running through fields in outlying farmlands. North Street curved northwards past the Parish Church of St. Nicholas and thence to London via Steyning. As Brighton expanded during the late 18th and early 19th centuries, agricultural crofts to the rear of buildings on West and North Streets were gradually developed into small scale streets and squares. During the 1810s and 1820s the land between the sea and Western Road was built up and from 1824 it became the main route to Brunswick Town. Had Robert Stephenson's "Natural Line" scheme for the London to Brighton railway been adopted, Brighton station would have been located behind Brunswick Square and the importance of Western Road would have been enhanced. From the 1820s development spread northwards from Western Road, which became the shopping centre for the area. Western Road extended further westwards into Hove with the onset of development there between 1871 and 1901. However, the Brighton-Hove boundary at Western Street does not delineate a change in architectural style: that is not apparent until Palmeira Square which separates the Regency work from the wide avenues of Victorian Hove.

10A Imperial Arcade
Imperial arcade was built in 1923 and refurbished in 1934 after the widening of Western Road in 1928. It is situated on a prominent location at the junction of North Street and Western Road and its design shows the unmistakable influence of Art Deco.

10B Churchill Square
Churchill Square was designed by Russell Diplock Associates in the early 1960s. Sir Hugh Casson, who was appointed in 1960 as adviser to the Corporation on planning proposals for Brighton central area and the sea-front, made recommendations for this large project amongst others. They were made in relation to issues of contextuality, height, profile, and the need to respect certain existing urban forms and important landmarks. He

10A A view up North Street towards Imperial Arcade.

10B The Sculpture of 'The Spirit of Brighton'.

cited Grenville Place and Russell Square as sensitive areas of some quality, and St. Paul's Church as an outstanding example of its period.

The site on which Churchill Square is located was covered originally by a number of small mews areas to the south, and Grenville Place to the north. During the nineteenth century the south side of Western Road was created from the gardens of Grenville Place to provide a shopping street. The first ideas for the development of the area were mooted by Brighton Corporation as early as 1935. The site area was increased by the ravages of bombing during the Second World War and parts lay derelict for some years.

Building work on Churchill Square was commenced in 1966. Regrettably Grenville Place was demolished to make way for the new scheme which consists of an extensive pedestrianised shopping precinct, offices bridging over it, a block of residential flats and a multi-level car park below. The shopping facility is well used and enjoyed by large numbers of people. It includes two supermarkets, a department store, three restaurants and many large and small popular shops. The hard edged mechanistic blocks of the 60s modern architecture were carefully thought out and detailed. Exposed aggregate concrete finishes, mosaic covered access towers, blue shaded panels to aluminium curtain walling were all designed with care and concern. Despite this thoroughness of attention to detail, the piazzas lack a proper sense of enclosure and are subject to through draughts whenever blustery conditions arise. The architectural language of the 60s was well used, but even the placing of free standing blocks and a large sculpture by William Mitchell to modulate the spaces failed to achieve the sense of enclosure of the much smaller Brighton Square (see 2F).

The 6.5 hectare site has a fall from north to south of 22 metres. This is resolved by a series of pedestrian levels leading down to the multi-storey car park, which has been described as unsympathetic to its surroundings. Of the three high rise blocks which were proposed originally, only one, Chartwell Court, was built. A residential block of 18 storeys finished in reddish-brown brick, it lacks the grace and finesse of Sussex heights (see 10E).

Today there may be more ingenious ways of dealing with this sort of complex problem, involving scale, size and mix of uses. However, Churchill Square is in many ways a great success, but perhaps there are certain problems which have arisen which at the time could not have been foreseen by the designers and are, in some respects, a result of the language they adopted for the scheme.

10C Russell Square with Sussex Heights dominating the skyline.

10C Clarence Square and Russell Square

Clarence Square and Russell Square are two of the very few examples of squares in Brighton sited in an inland location. Their development was doubtless due to the influence of late 18th century London squares, but on a much smaller scale.

Clarence Square was built from 1807 onwards. It was refaced with canted bays during the middle of the nineteenth century and has an early Victorian appearance similar to the northern side of Russell Square. The south and west sides of Russell Square were built between 1818 and 1825 and this is the early work of the younger Wilds. The square is long and narrow in form and is unfinished. The original facades are yellow brick, stuccoed at basement and ground floor, with double pilasters at first and second floor. There are timber balconies on brackets with canopies supported by delicate square tapered columns. The balustrading is ornate cast iron and the original French windows still exist at first floor.

10D The Royal Newburgh Assembly Rooms Cannon Place

The Royal Newburgh Assembly Rooms are on the corner of Cannon Place and St. Margaret's Place. They were designed and built around 1825 by Amon Henry Wilds and served for many years as a social meeting place for the west end of Brighton. The interior was converted in more recent years into residential accommodation. The exterior has been restored and redecorated. The facade to Cannon Place is double bow-fronted whilst the facade to St. Margaret's Place has a pedimented elevation. Its fine neo-classic portico, diastyle in antis, has attached columns and pilasters with interesting acanthus leafed capitals reminiscent of Adam. The coloured drawing of the original interior in the Pavilion Collection suggests that Wilds may have had a precedent in John Crunden's Assembly Rooms at the Castle Inn, the interior of which is now installed in St. Stephens Church, Montpelier Place (ref 11G).

10D The Royal Newburgh Assembly Rooms.

10E Sussex Heights
St. Margaret's Place

Sussex Heights was built on the site of St. Margaret's Chapel by A. H. Wilds which was demolished in 1959. This tower block of over a hundred residential units was designed by Richard Seifert and Partners in 1968 and built as part of the extension programme of the Metropole Hotel (9G). Hoteliers and residents regard it as an imposing and prestigious building and enjoy its luxury, convenience, and its unobstructed sea views. Conservationists, on the other hand, object to its intrusion on the skyline in what is predominantly a Regency area of Brighton. Sadly it has replaced the steeple of St. Pauls, West Street, as the most significant landmark in Brighton and it serves as a reminder of what might have occurred had the philosophy of comprehensive development of the 1960s been perpetuated.

10F Western Road Shops Woolworths, Primark, C & A and Macdonalds

10F Primark.

Woolworths, Primark (formerly Marks and Spencer) C & A and the building now occupied by Macdonalds, are the result of the development of Western Road after the road was widened in 1928. The typical 30s facades of Woolworths and C & A are regarded today with increased interest. These Art Deco, sub Assyrian style facades are now viewed more favourably than their 1960s equivalents. The contrast is typified by the present Marks and Spencer building with its exposed aggregate concrete facing panels, strip windows set in black marble, stainless steel clad columns, and marble fascia. Woolworths and C & A have facades which are symmetrical and have a centralised composition of motifs. Neither respond to their plans and are purely decorative. Woolworths is strictly a street facade while C & A is an island block and its facade becomes three dimensional as it is carried round to the side streets for a bay or so before the Deco is abandoned. Primark is Art Deco classical, while Macdonalds is a full 30s classical revival rendering.

10F Macdonalds.

10G Banks in Western Road

Two small bank buildings stand out as gems in Western Road. Midland Bank at No. 79 is a little overawed by its neighbours, but it is a delightful exercise in Edwardian Baroque dating from 1905. The buff sandstone facade is almost square and fronts a cubic banking hall. Three bays are formed by a pair of outer pilasters and a pair of inner half columns, all decorated with plain acanthus capitals. The grand central door is capped by an ornate pediment under an oval window. The executive architects were Gotch and Partners, but the original design is said to have been by Edwin Lutyens. This could be correct: Lutyens later designed three banks for the Midland in London and collaborated with Gotch in 1924 on the Head Office in Poultry. The National Westminster at No. 86 was built in 1925 and occupies the full end of the block between Preston Street and Sillwood Road. It is planned as a near perfect cube with triple bay facades on its three available elevations. Here plain Tuscan pilasters support a heavy cornice with balusters, and the arched openings have pronounced rustication, the outer pair carrying inset voussoirs in the manner of Palladio at Palazzo Inseppo Porto. The white portland stone looks a little cold and is not quite right for Brighton, but the design has been executed with impressive confidence.

10H Oriental Place and Sillwood Place

Oriental Place was part of a project for an oriental garden and a huge conservatory, the latter to be known as the Athenaeum. It was begun in 1825 and was originated by Henry Phillips who gave up teaching and from 1823 became actively engaged in horticulture and landscape gardening. The oriental garden was to be laid out on the site on which Sillwood Place now stands and the proposed conservatory in the centre was to be high enough to house tall trees and plants. In addition the Athenaeum was to include a literary institute comprising a library, a museum, a reading room and a school of science and learning. Oriental Place consists

10H The original scheme.

of two rows of houses leading from the seafront, and it was originally designed with terraces facing the sea. Lack of financial support caused the scheme to be abandoned in 1827. £20,000 was the sum required, but insufficient funds were raised to complete the houses in Oriental Place and Terrace or to carry out the garden. The half completed houses and the garden and Phillips' collection of plants were put up for sale. Sir David Scott, who had succeeded to a Baronetcy and to Sillwood Park Berkshire, and who had a house in Brighton, bought the unfinished scheme in 1827. He retained Amon Henry Wilds, who had worked with Henry Phillips as architect. Building work recommenced in late 1827 and Oriental Place was completed. It contains some of Wilds' best known details like the 'Ammonite' capitals and the semi circular shell motifs above first floor windows. Unfortunately the pilasters seem too large and the facade has a cramped appearance. The break forward given to the central composition and end pavilions is too little and the articulation is difficult to read visually. The inclusion of small pediments does nothing to relieve this and merely makes the centre third floor window an odd size. Only three houses of the eastern terrace were built thus forming Oriental Terrace which in 1864 was converted into the King's Hotel. Wilds was commissioned by Sir David Scott to build a house for his own occupation. This was called Sillwood House and it was located on the site of the ill fated oriental garden and Athenaeum. Today it provides storage space for the neighbouring department store. The space between Sillwood House, which Sir David Scott occupied briefly, and Oriental Place was laid out by Wilds as Sillwood Place. The eastern side only remains today. A modern residential block built in the 1970s occupies the western side to Montpelier Road. The area now called Sillwood Road was originally the stables and servants area of Sillwood House.

10J Western Terrace and Western Pavilion
Western Terrace is a small cul-de-sac off Western Road. It lies to the north east of the boundary of the estate. Some delightful buildings are to be seen in the Terrace, all built at the same date but in three different styles.

When Sillwood House was being built the younger Wilds connected it with Gothic House, constructed a few years earlier by Amon Wilds and Charles Busby, by inserting a row of five neo-classic houses designed as a most relaxed and attractive ensemble. They are of stucco with fluted columns and a variety of capitals, including the ammonite and anthemion. In 1833 Wilds built for his own occupation No. 9 Western Terrace, known as Western Pavilion. It is a sort of miniature version of the Royal Pavilion complete with dome and Hindu details including multiple cusped Saracenic arches and tiny minarets. Originally both facing houses at the north end of Sillwood Place were in oriental style and are about the same date. One only remains on the eastern side.

10J The Western Pavilion.

10K Gothic House
Debenham's Store, Western Road

Gothic House, built between 1822 and 1825 by Wilds and Busby, was initially No. 1 Western Terrace, but was converted later into three dwellings. It is not early Gothic Revival but Gothick (Georgian Gothic) and their only known work in the style. It is still pluralistic and fanciful with the mediaeval scholarship of Pugin and Ruskin still a few years away. A Gothic extension to the north facade was executed in 1880 by W. H. Stevens and included were five bow fronted houses to the west. The conversion into a shop took place in 1898. Later, in 1920, most of the Western Terrace houses were also incorporated. There is sufficient of the original fabric in Western Terrace and Western Road above the shop fronts to visualise how Gothic House with its crocketed pinnacles and tracery was meant to appear. The younger Wilds may have financed the whole of Western Terrace himself, which could relate to him living and working in most of the houses at different times.

10L Christchurch Montpelier
Two Piers Housing Co-operative
Montpelier Road
This is a new urban infill scheme on a site between Regency facades, which was originally occupied by a Wagner church. The church was consecrated in 1838 and demolished in 1982. Michael Blee's new building is a fittingly apt replacement for the rudimentary 13th century Gothic style structure. It is a co-operative housing scheme comprising two blocks, one of which continues the Regency facades fronting Montpelier Road, whilst the other faces smaller Regency facades on Bedford Place. Both blocks house four single parent families at ground level with shared accommodation for thirty-one young people on the upper floors. In addition the Montpelier Road accommodation provides for three wheelchair disabled units and a laundry.

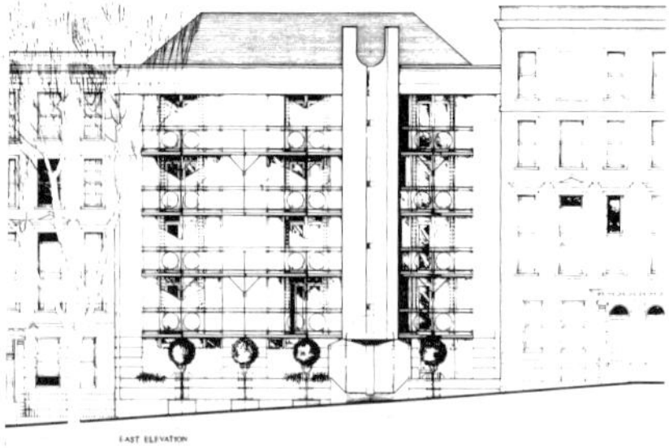

10L Two Piers Housing.

The disposition of internal elements is where the design displays its mastery of the problem. Within the smaller inner courtyard a communal room lies on the route of the 'street' which links Montpelier Road and Bedford Place. Cast iron columns which once supported the church balconies have been re-used along this route. The shared accommodation has been given an open galleried system of access made possible by continuous balconies and escape stairs on the street facades which seek to retain Regency tradition of formality and decorum. The inner facades are, in contrast, informal with a vocabulary of pitched roofs and cedar cladding. Internally, fairfaced blockwork and rugged detailing in a "monastic" tradition allows for super-imposition of individual but independent decor.

10M Church School/Theatre
Bedford Place

The Reverend James Vaughan, the first Perpetual Curate of Christchurch Montpelier Road, built a minature Tudor Gothic Sunday School in 1841 in Bedford Place adjoining the church. The original single storey structure has well detailed window bays faced with flint cobbles. The cornice, quoins and window surrounds are stucco and there are Dutch gables above the outer window bays. A large red brick extension was built behind it in the 1900s and has marred the original building. Since the 1970s the School has been used as a ballet school and theatre.

10N St. Andrew's Chapel
Waterloo Street

St. Andrew's was not part of the Brunswick Town Estate, but served as a chapel of ease for its residents. The land on which it stands was bought by the Reverend Edward Everard when Brunswick Town was being built. Everard commissioned Charles Barry to design the new church. Charles Barry, a gifted but unknown architect, had won the competition held in 1824 for the design of St. Peter's in Valley Gardens (see 3L). He was appointed to design the Sussex County Hospital (see 8H) about the same time, possibly through Everard's influence as he was a joint Secretary of the Hospital.

St. Andrew's was built between 1827 and 1828. St. Peter's took four years to complete so that, almost simultaneously, there were two churches by Barry being consecrated. St. Peter's was a Gothick Chapel in Portland Stone and St. Andrew's Chapel in brickwork and render, Italianate by way of France and the Rationalists. The detailing is influenced by the Quattrocento, particularly the main doorway and the bell tower openings. The original chapel consisted of the nave only. The Chancel was added in 1882 by Charles Barry's son. Originally the church also accommodated a school in a small narrow room at the side. The Chapel became most fashionable and in the early years titled people were often to be seen in the congregation. The Rev. Edward Everard ministered there for ten years. The Church was successfully renovated in 1922 by W. R. Blacking who was also responsible for the design of the Baldachino. Today the church stands empty and unused.

10N St. Andrew's Chapel.

10P Upper Market Street and Lower Market Street

Upper and Lower Market Streets were built as part of Brunswick Town by Wilds and Busby in 1828. They were separated by the Market and are good examples of smaller scale streets built for tradesmen and other working people of Brunswick Town. Other streets with service accommodation were Brunswick Street East and Brunswick Street West, which were mews behind the Square and Terraces. They included coach housing, stables and residential accommodation over for coachmen. Worth noting are numbers 10-13.

10Q Old Market Arts Centre Upper Market Street

Brunswick Town was built as a self-contained estate, but no shops were permitted within its curtilage. Shopping facilities were provided in 1828 by the creation of Brunswick Market, a large building located behind Brunswick Square to the east. It carried on trading for several years selling various sorts of provisions. As shopping developed in Western Road the need for the Market decreased and by 1839 it was being used as a school. Later it became the locally famous Dupont's Riding School. In the 1960s it was occupied by a wholesale grocery firm and by the late 1970s it had become an Arts Centre for Hove. The east side of the building is the original Market elevation, but the north elevation is a Victorian addition.

10S The Wick Inn Western Road

The Wick public house occupies the site of the old thatched building which served as the ale house to eastern Hove. The site opposite was the original Hove cricket ground which doubtless boosted its trade.

The existing facade dating from 1873 has decorative capitals of flowers and fir cones which enclose the Victorian etched glass advertising the various antidotes sold within.

10S The Wick Inn.

10T Maples Store Western Road

The building now occupied by Maples was formerly Palmeira Stores, opened in 1873 by the Brighton and Hove Co-operative Supply Association. It is neo-classic with the flavour of the Second Empire. An Italian palace third or fourth removed, it is on four floors and the balconied windows on the south facing main elevation have articulated arcades of attached columns in pairs. It occupies a site on which the unfinished Palmeira Hotel stood for some years and it is thought that this may have been incorporated into the present building which has more the appearance of a hotel than a shop. The Association sold all types of provisions and goods to members at economic prices. The facilities included a reading room which adjoined the refreshment salon on the first floor.

10U Pickfords Repository Holland Road

Pickfords Repository was designed originally as an annexe to Palmeira Stores. The architects were Thomas Lainson and Son and it was built for the Co-operative Supply Association in 1893. The style is Second Empire with some Queen Anne trimmings. It was built for storage, of furniture, of plate, of general goods and included stabling for horses and housing for vans. Pickfords took it over in 1950 and moved the memorial stone recording the date and architect's name from the gateway to the internal courtyard.

11 MONTPELIER & THE SEVEN DIALS

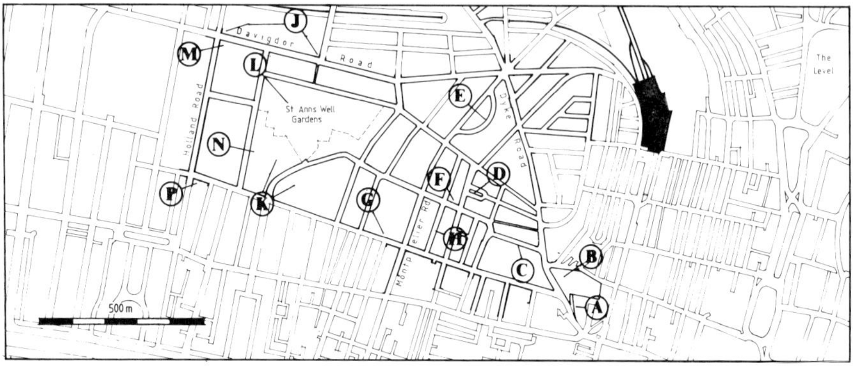

The area contained between Western Road and the Shoreham Railway Line and stretching westwards from Queen's Road towards The Drive in Hove might be loosely described as Victorian insofar that most of it was developed after the accession of Queen Victoria and before the First World War. However, the variety of architectural styles which it contains bear witness to the inventiveness of that period. Within it are a number of separate and distinctive communities. The Montpelier district grew up after the opening of the railway to London at that moment when it first became thinkable to work in the capital and live beside the sea in Brighton. At the time the new houses stood on the edge of the Downs and enjoyed views of sea and countryside. Seven Dials, a busy junction where seven roads meet, is one of a number of node points which have become landmarks in Brighton and has given its name to an area which grew up during the mid 1800s. As the century progressed so development moved westwards to encompass the area round St. Anne's Well Gardens.

11A Wykeham Terrace

This attractive terrace of Regency Gothic houses was built in 1830. In 1855 a part of the terrace was linked through to adjoining properties in Queen's Square to become St. Mary's Home for Female Penitents, and institution set up by George Wagner to rehabilitate reformed prostitutes.

11B St. Nicholas's Church
Church Street

St. Nicholas's Church stood on raised ground outside of the original rectangle of the old town. The present buildings date from the 14th century though a church on this site was recorded in the Domesday Book of 1086. A beautifully preserved font of that period shows the Last Supper and scenes from the life of St. Nicholas. Before the opening of the Chapel Royal (5R) in 1795, St. Nicholas's was Brighton's only church. During the early part of the 19th century new churches appeared in the more fashionable east end of the town and the buildings suffered neglect. In 1835 T. W. Horsefield described the church to be "in all respects far below mediocrity", and in 1853 the vicar, Henry Michell Wagner, commissioned Richard Cromwell Carpenter to supervise restorations. Carpenter was over-zealous and rebuilt so much of the original church that today only the flint tower, the chancel arch and the nave arcades can truly be dated to the 14th century. The churchyard contains a number of interesting tombstones. One marks the grave of Nicholas Tettersell who engineered the escape of Charles II from Brighton to France following the Battle of Worcester in 1651 and who is also remembered for his persecution of the town's

11B St. Nicholas's Church.

Quakers. Another records that Martha Gunn, who died in 1815 at the age of 88, was "peculiarly distinguished as a bather in this Town for nearly 70 years". Phoebe Hessel, who died in 1821, is said to have concealed her sex in order to serve as a soldier in the 5th Regiment of Foot. At the east end of the churchyard there is a large tomb decorated with shell ornaments designed by Amon Henry Wilds as a memorial to his father, the architect Amon Wilds.

11C Clifton Terrace

The houses of Clifton Terrace enjoy a commanding view of the sea from their upper windows and share a communal garden square. Built during the 1850s, they offer an interesting hybrid of the Regency and Victorian styles with possibly the latest examples of Brighton's characteristic bay windows with bonnet-like canopies.

11D Powis Square

Powis Square was built during the 1850s and remains one of the few enclosed inland squares of Brighton. In style and scale it is comparable with contemporary developments on the seafront. The elevations are late Georgian in inspiration with bowed fronts on 3 storeys. Small pediments bear witness to a Victorian revival of Palladian details.

11E Montpelier Crescent

This grand crescent was developed before 1845 by Amon Henry Wilds. It comprises large linked mansions each originally containing a pair of houses under pediments with ammonite capitals topping the pilasters. The crescent was built in stages, Nos. 1-6 and 34-38 being of a later date which explains the overall lack of consistency.

11F St. Michael's Church
Victoria Road

The Church of St. Michael and All Angels looks a little out of place in Montpelier: it is a red brick building in an area of stucco a decidedly mid-Victorian building in an area which is early-Victorian. Perhaps it is for this reason tht it has been described as "a back street church with town centre status". In fact,

11F St. Michael's Church.

it is really two churches. The first was designed by G. F. Bodley and opened in 1862. It is built of red brick with sandstone coursing and is an interesting example of mid-century revival gothic. There is a rich interior with polychrome brickwork reminiscent of Butterfield. The new church proved to be too small and an extension was designed by William Burges in 1868 in the form of a second nave to the north of the first. This extension was eventually built in 1895 after Burges's death, and is a particularly fine example of 13th century pastiche on a grand scale with soaring brick-vaulted nave, triforium and clerestory. The whole church now measures 30 metres by 33 metres. The stained glass in the western window of Bodley's original nave and the smaller windows in the east and west ends of the south aisle are from the firm of William Morris and are among the earliest examples of their ecclesiastical work. Morris was also responsible with Webb for the painted roof over the sanctuary. The altar in the south chapel was moved from the Church of All Saints in Compton Avenue after its demolition in the 1950s. The interiors of this strange double church are particularly interesting and it is sad that the building is often closed to the public.

11G St. Stephen's Church
Montpelier Place

St. Stephen's Church actually started its life as the ballroom of the Castle Inn a mile away to the east of its present location. In 1766 the architect John Crunden was responsible for building the new Assembly Rooms which were added to the eastern side of the Castle Inn (see 2A) overlooking the Steine. Crunden was a pupil of Henry Holland the elder and his interiors were designed in the Rococo style popularised by Robert Adam. The ballroom was a double cube measuring 24 metres by twelve and decorated with delicately worked Corinthian pilasters. The Castle Hotel was bought by George IV who annexed it to the southern wing of the Royal Pavilion. In 1822 the ballroom was converted into a private chapel for the King's own use. Later in 1850 the Pavilion was acquired by the town and the southern wing was demolished to allow for the widening of North Street. The royal chapel, however, was saved from demolition and moved to its present site where it was installed behind a rather plain classical facade. Astonishingly Crunden's interiors have survived though they are now in poor condition. The building is no longer used as a church and now serves as a day centre for the homeless.

11G St. Stephen's Church.

11H Montpelier Villas

Montpelier Villas were designed by Amon Henry Wilds in 1845 towards the end of his career and are in the style of the late Regency. Each "villa" consists of a pair of semi-detached houses with entrances placed discreetly on the side elevation. The piano nobile and basement are finished in heavily rusticated stucco, while the upper floor is plain, apart from the rusticated corner quoins. The eaves are supported on bold brackets which alternate with medallions. Each house is given a bow window under a bonnet canopy with a curved wrought iron railing. The houses have suffered few alterations and are well maintained and the street looks much as it must have done when it was first built.

11J Office Buildings
Davigdor Road

A series of new office developments have been built along the north side of Davigdor Road as part of improvements to what was an area of industry. The Legal and General Assurance Society occupies an elegantly converted building on the corner of Davigdor and Montefiore Roads. The original building had been built in 1904 as a furniture warehouse to serve Hannington's Store. The conversion was carried out by the firm of Devereux and Partners in 1972. The original arched brick facades have been carefully restored and modern glass inserted within them. Next door is an uncompromising modern development designed by the APP Partnership. This was built in two phases. The first phase, Preece House, contains 2,300 square metres of lettable space and was completed in 1978. The second, Ewbank House, is a glass fronted tower block with twice the floor area and was completed in 1983. The whole development provides a typical example of modern office building, marred mainly by the absence of landscaping. Nearby the offices of TSB occupy another converted warehouse. The architects for the conversion were again the APP Partnership. This yellow brick building had been quite dilapidated and it has been impressively restored and integrated within a modern glass shell. Spitfire House is a new office building completed in 1986. This is a peculiar brick building designed in what passes for a vernacular style. The result relates badly to its surroundings and looks more like a block of flats than a block of offices.

11J The Legal and General.

11K Furze Court and Wick Hall
Furze Hill

These two massive, brick-built blocks of flats were built in 1936 and provide an interesting example of luxury flat design of the period. The site had been previously occupied by Wick Hall, a large house designed by Decimus Burton for Isaac Lyon Goldsmid in 1833, which was finally demolished in 1935. The flats boasted every modern convenience and were heated from a single central boiler. A restaurant was included in the original development, though this no longer exists.

11L St. Anne's Well Gardens

This park originally formed a part of the Wick Estate, a large landholding which once stretched from Preston Village to the coast. The estate was assembled by the Staply family after 1573 and was bought by a Brighton brewing family called Scutt in 1701. Chalybeate springs were discovered in 1750 and, having received Dr. Russell's seal of approval, became immensely popular with visitors. The estate was sold off by the Reverend Thomas Scutt during the 1820s. One part of it was developed after 1825 as Brunswick Town, while the remainder, including the site for Wick House, was bought by Isaac Lyon Goldsmid. In 1850 Goldsmid laid out the 6 acres of St. Anne's Well Gardens beside Wick House. After 1894 the gardens were leased to George Albert Smith, an early pioneer of the cinema, who used them in the shooting of a number of his films.

In 1908 the gardens were acquired by the Council and opened to the public. Many of the original buildings were removed, and in 1935 the nineteenth century well house was demolished, the springs having all but dried up. In 1954 a garden for the blind was opened.

11M Unigate Dairies
Davigdor Road

This building for Unigate Dairies was designed by Clayton and Black in the late 1920s. It is an interesting example of the Art Deco style. The centralised composition, with raised front parapet between scrolls, the suggestion of a pediment over the three part window, the narrow and wide banded Art Deco glazing, and the two tone cream faience facing slabs are a well chosen use of a vocabulary which became current for new factories, cinemas and garages in the 20s and 30s. The first example of the style used in this country was probably Michelin House in Brompton Road, London, built in 1911. The most famous essays were probably the Hoover factory and the Firestone factory, now sadly demolished, on the Great West Road in London. In Brighton the Savoy, (see 2B); the Essoldo, (see 5P) and Caffyn's Garage (see 14N) were all built in this style. Unlike the buildings of the International Modern Movement this version of modern design carried no underlying social message. Here for example, the decorative motif of a milk bottle within a red triangle simply warns of the dangers of drinking unpasteurized milk. The shift in taste over the last thirty years has brought this modernistic building into the listings as a building of historic importance.

11N Park Gate
Somerhill Road

The architect Eric Lyons challenged the professional codes of his day and created his own development company to which he gave the name 'Span'. Lyons was convinced that property developers actively discouraged good design and that they prevented architects from offering the public modern houses at prices they could afford. Span successfully developed a number of housing schemes mainly in South London and Lyons went on to be elected President of the RIBA. Park Gate Flats in Somerhill Road were designed by Lyons with Geoffrey Townsend in 1960 and built by Span. The development contains 47 flats arranged on four floors around a communal

11N The Internal Courtyard of Park Gate.

courtyard and uses vertical tile cladding. The landscaping is less impressive than in other Span developments and the flat roofs have proved difficult to maintain.

11P Synagogue
Lansdowne Road

Built in 1938 to designs by Edward Lewis, this small synagogue is an interesting example of pre-war architecture showing a strong hint of Viennese Jugendstil.

11P Synagogue.

12 MOULSECOOMB & THE NORTH EAST

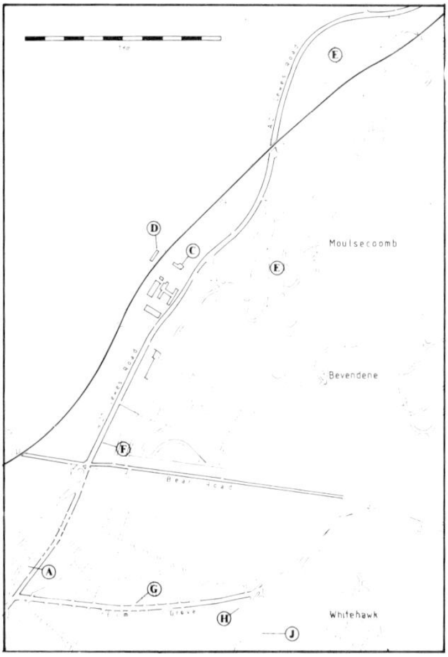

Today, a dominant feature of the area is the new traffic interchange recently completed below Bear Road. It incorporates a supermarket with car-park which externally attempts to reflect local Victorian industrial architecture. The supermarket is well used and full of activity, but the island with its petrol station is totally cut off by the flow of traffic.

12A St. Martins Church
Lewes Road

St. Martins Church was built in the middle of the 1870s as a memorial to the Reverend Henry Michell Wagner by his three sons. It was Arthur Wagner's second great church project and it was built to seat 1,500 of the faithful, and was wholly free of rented pews. The Church was sited in Lewes Road and as it served the needs of Preston Barracks, where a cavalry regiment was regularly stationed, it was named after the soldier saint, St. Martin. The design of the church was entrusted to Somers Clarke jnr. the son of a local solicitor who was a close friend of the Rev. Henry Michell Wagner. Somers Clarke jnr. was a

Moulsecoomb is believed to have derived its name from Mul, the brother of a King of the Saxons. Mul is best known for his laying waste the kingdom of Kent and for being burnt with several followers as an act of retaliation by the men of Kent. Molstan, or Mul's stone, according to the Domesday Book, appears to be a boundary mark in the Falmer Hundred. It was referred to as Mouliscombe, meaning Moul, his valley, by William second Earl of Surrey.

Moulsecoomb was never a village and has no church and for centuries was simply a farm hamlet in a downland valley through which passed the road from Brighton to Lewes. Its only building of note is Moulsecoomb Place.

Between the wars two large new housing estates were built at Moulsecoomb. This was subsequent to the clearance by the Corporation of large areas of bad housing near the centre of the town. Other estates were built at Whitehawk and Manor Farm. The layouts of North and South Moulsecoomb are two of the best examples in the country of local authority housing built in that era.

12A St. Martin's today.

12A St. Martin's as originally conceived.

pupil in the 1860s of Sir George Gilbert Scott and from 1876-1892 he was in partnership with J. T. Micklethwaite. During those years Somers Clarke produced some of the finest Victorian churches in southern England. He was an unusual character who, for reasons of health, spent much time in Egypt. St. Martins was his first major work and possibly his finest as a consequence of working with the Wagners whose artistic taste, architectural vision and unlimited generosity were decisive factors in the development of the design. The yellow and red brickwork describes an almost ruthless essay in 13th century Gothic with pinnacle capped buttresses at the west and east ends and tall lancet windows. Yet the interior has a stunning beauty greatly enhanced by the omission of screens, and the beautiful proportion of the space is given unity by the internal fittings which also were designed by the architect. Wood for the parquet floor was brought back from the Mount of Olives by one of the late vicar's sons (and it was the first example of its use in a church). Sadly the Church never got the saddleback tower included in the original design which would have given the building a far greater presence.

12C The Hall House.

12C Moulsecoomb Place and Hall House

The Hall House to the rear of Moulsecoomb Place is the oldest surviving building in Brighton. It was probably built between 1350 and 1400 during the reign of Edward III. In 1639 records show that the old cottage at Moulsecoomb was seized by one Edward Culpepper. Moulsecoomb Place appears to be an early 19th century seven bay house in yellow brick, but behind the facade is a farm house dating back to the early 18th century. The work was done by Benjamin Tillstone who purchased Moulsecoomb Farm and turned it into his country house. Apparently the Prince Regent often stayed there, sleeping in the room above the drawing room, and up the hill the dovecote was converted into a summer house for him where he would play his silver flute, given to him by Tillstone. In return the Prince gave him three huge mahogany doors, possibly from Grove House. The recess in the wall to the south of the house was used as a sentry box during his visits.

12D Moulsecoomb Railway Station.

12D Moulsecoomb Railway Station

The new British Rail Station on the Lewes to Brighton line is sited on the slope behind the Hall House. It was designed by the Chief Architect's Department, British Rail Southern Region, which is a progressive office with a growing reputation for innovative design.

Moulsecoomb Station consists of two small buildings and a bridge. Both buildings are built of timber and well detailed, in part to deter vandalism. The station serves the main campus of Brighton Polytechnic — a collection of utilitarian modern buildings which straddle the Lewes Road.

12E Moulsecoomb Housing Estates

During the inter-war years Moulsecoomb Valley became the site for two large housing estates, North Moulsecoomb and South Moulsecoomb, and the Moulsecoomb Farm buildings were demolished. The houses were described as "fit for heroes" by the planners of the twenties and the estates were hailed as the "Utopia of Moulsecoomb". They were built to accommodate the housing shortages following the First World War and also to provide new council houses for those needing rehousing subsequent to the clearance of bad housing areas in central Brighton. They embody in their layout and house types the development of garden city principles, and also the effects of planning legislation in that period. North Moulsecoomb is cited as one of the best examples of local authority housing schemes in this country built during the 20s and 30s and has been studied by planners from all over the world. It was designed by Professor Adshead.

For many people who had suffered life in the bad housing conditions of central Brighton, the new homes in this setting offered a welcome contrast. There have been two problems in recent years: first, a general decline brought on by lack of maintenance and second, a severe lack of services catering for the needs of residents. Recent attempts to improve services to the area include a new railway station (ref 12D), giving a direct link to the centre of Brighton.

12F The Tram Depot
Lewes Road

The long history of Brighton's various public transport companies came together with the formation, in 1884, of the Brighton, Hove and Preston United Omnibus Company Limited. In the previous year Magnus Volk had obtained from the Corporation a six month licence to experiment with his electric railway car on a 2′ 0″ gauge track on the seafront. In 1885 a converted horse car began work on a 3′ 6″ gauge tramway between Brighton and Shoreham. The venture proved successful and was said to have achieved speeds of 20 mph. The Board of Trade at the time was adamant in its view that 6 mph was enough for anybody.

Brighton's policy with regard to the tramway undertaking was that it should be self-contained and therefore offices, sheds and workshops should be built in one place under the auspices of the Tramway's Engineer. The Corporation Tramway Depot and Workshops were established in 1901 in Coombe Terrace, Lewes Road. The brick administration block is still in use today on the northern end of the site. This building still advertises itself with a few remaining windows etched with the Brighton Coat of Arms and the words "Brighton Corporation Tramways". All of the eighty quality cars that were running in 1935 were constructed and maintained in the Department's own workshops.

12E The Moulsecoomb Estates.

12G St. Wilfred's Elm Grove.

12G St. Wilfred's Elm Grove

St. Wilfred's Elm Grove was designed in 1932 and built in 1933-34 by H. S. Goodhart-Rendel (see 5S). Goodhart-Rendel was a scholar with enormous interest in and enthusiasm for 19th century architecture. He was trained by a church architect, Sir Charles Nicholson, and had very strong views on church design which were incorporated in his work. St. Wilfred's is an essay in the expression of structure within a developed style of Rational Eclecticism. Goodhart-Rendel used intricate two-toned brickwork and geometric form, which might appear to have an affinity with contemporary continental expressionist work. But his church was more in common with the work of Mackintosh or the late churches of Richard Norman Shaw than with some of the churches of his contemporaries. He strove to achieve sight lines so that every member of the congregation might have a clear view of the altar. The solution lay in having a wide nave and narrow passage aisles. The altar is side lit and set on a blank wall to avoid glare. The structure is uncompromisingly modern and is made up of 9″ brick double walls in lime mortar, supporting a reinforced concrete roof intended to be fireproof. The church is neither 30s Modern Movement nor is it a piece of historic representation. It combines functional clarity with a highly selective taste. Its present state is one of immediate concern.

12H Brighton General Hospital.

12J The New Race Stand of 1852.

12H Brighton General Hospital
Elm Grove

The Brighton Act of 1810 provided for the appointment of Directors and Guardians of the Poor of Brighton. It also laid down their responsibilities for instituting workhouses. A site was selected and purchased on Race Hill in 1853 for the construction of a new and larger workhouse. Work began in 1865 on the building which had a front elevation 95 metres long and 15 metres high to the eaves. The design was plain except for four gables and a clock tower bearing the Brighton Coat of Arms and the date 1866. The building incorporated a well contrived natural ventilation system using a series of cast iron grills in the corridors at each level.

In 1915 the military authorities took over the building and its name was changed to the Kitchener Indian Hospital. It was staffed by doctors and surgeons from the Indian services and succoured 2,000 Indian male patients.

After the First World War the hospital reverted to being a Poor Law Institution, caring for largely destitute ex-servicemen who could not find work. In 1935 it was renamed the Brighton General Hospital and shook off its ties with Poor Law and the Workhouse. Today the Brighton General Hospital and the Royal Sussex County Hospital form a major provincial District General Hospital. A full range of medical and surgical facilities are provided, including a number of highly specialised units.

12J Brighton Racecourse

Horse racing began in Brighton 200 years ago when officers of the Army Militia, who were stationed in the town, raced against one another. The sport was officially recognised on Whitehawk Hill in 1783 at the time of the Prince Regent's first visit. The original grandstand was built in 1788. In 1803, after only a few years of use during which the roof was robbed of its lead several times, it was accidentally burned down by the caretaker. The local inhabitants from miles around saw the fire and believed that Napoleon's men had landed and were burning and sacking the town. Brighton races remained under royal patronage until 1816. The Prince would drive in a barouche drawn by six grey mares from the Old Steine to the starting post and would later present the trophies. Illness and affairs of state prevented his attending after 1816 and the Races lost popularity, recovering only after the arrival of the railway in 1841.

Brighton Races grew in popularity during the late 19th century and into the 20th. In 1938 a new Members and Tattersalls Enclosure was built at a cost of £77,000. In 1965 a new stand and restaurant were built, enabling 5,200 seated spectators to watch the races in comfort.

12J Brighton Racecourse.

13 PRESTON & PATCHAM

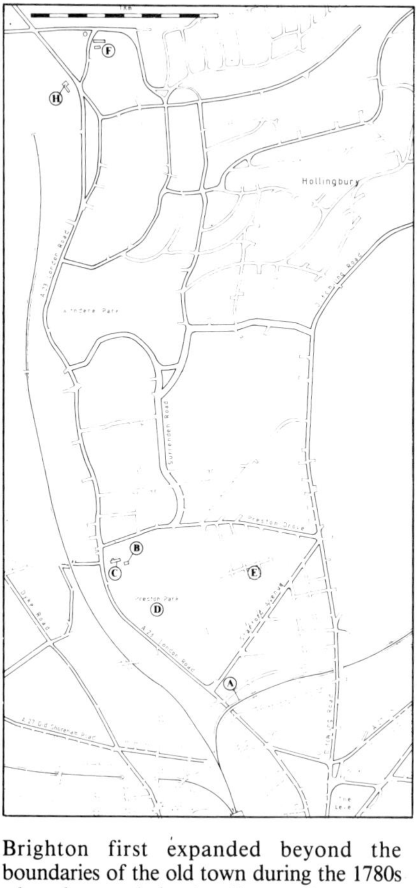

Brighton first expanded beyond the boundaries of the old town during the 1780s when the population hardly exceeded 3,500. The town's popularity as a resort led to a twentyfold increase of population during the next 60 years, much of it accommodated in new developments on the town's former laines. The 30 years following the opening of the railway in 1841 saw a further doubling of the population from 45,000 to 90,000, much of the physical expansion being accommodated on land to the east and west of the central area. In 1854 Brighton successfully petitioned for incorporation as a Borough with boundaries enclosing 1,100 hectares. At this time expansion northwards was limited by the landholdings of the Standford Estate, a swathe of land stretching from the Ditchling Road in the east to what is now Hove's seafront. The estate had been purchased by William Stanford in 1794. His son, William Stanford II, died in 1853 leaving the estate to his daughter, Ellen, who was still a minor. Her fortune was put into a trust, a fact which complicated the subsequent sale and development of the estate. Stanford land first started to be developed during the 1870s following Ellen's marriage in 1867. Large villas were built along Preston Road north of the viaduct, and Preston's railway station opened in 1875. During the next 20 years the land lying between Preston Park and Fiveways was developed as a homogeneous Victorian suburb. Further developments followed along the northern axis of the Preston valley and soon Patcham Village was linked to Brighton by a continuous ribbon of development. In 1928 the borough boundaries were officially extended, increasing the area of the town from 4 square miles to almost 18 square miles, and Patcham Village was incorporated into the Borough of Brighton.

13A London Road Viaduct and Station

The main rail link to London was completed in 1841 (see 5A). Such was the popularity of rail travel that plans for branch lines to east and west were immediately put into effect. Rennie's chosen location for Brighton's main railway station at the head of Queen's Road was 40 metres above sea level, and the line to Lewes had to bridge over the London Road. A viaduct was chosen in preference to an embankment which, although cheaper to build, would have obstructed one of the town's major thoroughfares and obliterated a number of houses. Objectors to the viaduct argued that it would be expensive, and that it would be vulnerable to enemy attack. They were proved correct on the latter score almost a century later in 1943 when a German air raid destroyed two of the arches. The damage was repaired immediately and the line re-opened within 4 hours.

The viaduct took only ten months to complete, though it contained over ten million bricks: a laying rate of one brick per second. It is 400 yards long and consists of 26 lesser arches, each one spanning 9 metres, with one main arch across London Road spanning 15 metres at a height of 20 metres above ground. It was considered to be a major engineering feat in its day, and it is still regarded as one of the finest monuments of early railway

13A London Road Viaduct.

architecture. When it opened in 1846 it was on the edge of open country and one commentator compared it to an aquaduct in one of Claude Lorraine's classical landscapes!

The spread of suburban Brighton during the following decades led to a demand for intermediate stations. London Road Station at the eastern end of the viaduct was opened in 1877. It was built by W. Sawyer at a cost of £3,944 and is in the Italianate style favoured by railway architects of the day.

13B Preston Church
Preston Drove

Little now remains of the village of Preston, referred to as Prestetone in the Domesday Book, and swallowed up during the 19th century expansion of Brighton. The original site is crossed by the London Road and to the west a few houses from the late 17th century survive in the midst of later Victorian development. To the east on higher ground are the parish church and the manor house.

The church of St. Peter dates in its present form from the 13th century though two earlier churches had existed on the site. The main walls are of flint with stone dressings and are pierced by Early English lancet windows. The church was famous for its frescoes which were rediscovered in almost perfect condition in 1830 having been covered by plaster since the time of Henry VIII. One scene depicts the murder of Thomas A Becket, which might explain why they were painted over. In 1906 a fire destroyed the roof of the nave and the frescoes were badly damaged; today only three fragments remain. The chancel is covered by an interesting barrel roof. The chancel stalls are finely carved with a variety of figures, including a Red Indian and his Squaw, said to be the work of Grindling Gibbons.

13B Preston Church.

13C Preston Manor
Preston Drove
A building has existed on the site of Preston Manor for as long as there has been a church beside it. In 1738 the core of the present buildings was raised on the foundations of the previous mediaeval structure by Thomas Western, Lord of the Manor. This house was sold in 1794 with its surrounding estates of almost 400 hectares to William Stanford, the son of one of Western's tenants. The Stanfords became a powerful family during the 19th century partly as a result of the fact that their lands blocked the further expansion of Brighton towards the north. Stanford's granddaughter, Ellen Fane-Bennet Stanford, sold land for the development of the Preston Estate (see 13E) during the last decades of the 19th century. In 1883 the town was able to acquire the land immediately to the south of the manor to create the open space now known as Preston Park (see 13D). In 1905 the Stanford family employed the architect Charles Stanley Peach to remodel the existing house and to add on an extra wing of accommodation to the west, thus creating the substantial Edwardian house which stands today. In 1933, with the death of Sir Charles Stanford, Ellen Stanford's second husband, the house passed to the town and was opened to the public as a museum. From the main approach the house appears as a rather plain symmetrical front of 5 bays on two principal floors above a basement, with the later 1906 wing on the right. The garden front reveals a flavour of Brighton with its collection of balconies and bays. The interiors are still open to the public and offer a rare glimpse of Edwardian family life.

13C Preston Manor.

13D Preston Park
Preston Road
In 1883 Brighton Corporation bought 10 hectares of open parkland from the Stanford family for the sum of £50,000, thus saving it from building development. The purchase was made possible through a bequest of £70,000 from William Edmund Davies, a wealthy bookmaker and racehorse owner who had died in 1879. The land lay to the immediate south of Preston Manor in the bottom of Preston Valley, and included a cricket field and an area to the west of the main London Road known as the Rookeries.

In 1884 Preston Park, as it came to be known, was officially opened to the public. In 1887 the building known as the chalet was constructed, and with it a cycle track, at the time a very novel attraction! In 1881 a clock-tower, designed in the Flemish Renaissance style by Francis May, the Borough Engineer, was erected. Further improvements were carried out in 1928, when a pavilion was built with bowling greens, tennis courts and a rose garden. The rotunda which now stands nearby was originally built as part of the Wembley Exhibition of 1924, and was moved to Brighton in 1929. In 1933 the Rookeries were transformed into a charming rock garden complete with artificial streams and waterfalls, using 1,350 tons of imported Cheddar Stone. During the Second World War Preston Park was dug up to serve as food producing allotments, but was later reinstated. Today it offers a much appreciated recreational space and remains as a fine example of a Victorian municipal park.

13D Clock Tower, Preston Park.

13E Preston Park Housing
Stanford Avenue

Ellen Stanford began to release land for development only after her marriage to Vere Fane-Bennet in 1867 (see 13 and 13C). The trust which administered her estate imposed strict controls on the form and quality of development. The area bounded today by the Lewes branch line, Ditchling Road, Preston Drove and Preston Park was set out to a street plan with Stanford Avenue acting as a main spine running up the contours towards Fiveways and serving lateral streets which ran along the contours. Blocks of land were released to builders on temporary leases, and individual freeholds could only be sold to prospective house-buyers if the development had achieved the prescribed standards. In some roads substantial villas were permitted, on others compact two storeyed terraced houses. In this way a whole suburb was developed to a uniform pattern over a period of about 20 years. The estate catered for a mixture of social classes and included several churches, a number of shopping clusters and one substantial school. It is still today an interesting example of a late Victorian suburban development. The triangle formed by Stanford Avenue, Southdown Avenue and Grantham Road was built during the 1890s and offers a cross-section of the whole estate. The Stanford Avenue houses are spacious detached and semi-detached villas decorated with terracotta reliefs and mosaic pathways and set in generous gardens. In Southdown Avenue the houses are more modest and semi-detached though they still carry decorative features. The Grantham Road houses are narrow fronted and terraced. These distinctions were imposed almost a century ago by the original landowner, but they are still reflected today in the prices of houses and the pattern of occupation. The centre of the triangle served originally as a pasture for the carriage horses of the Stanford Avenue residents, but is now occupied by garages.

13E Terrace Houses in Edburton Road.

13E Houses in Southdown Avenue.

13F Patcham Village

The village of Patcham dates back at least to Saxon times. It is one of several villages which were swallowed up by the Victorian and inter-war expansion of Brighton and officially incorporated within the Borough under the boundary changes of 1928. At this time the new "Gateway to Brighton" was marked on the road to London with the construction of a pair of massive stone pylons at Pyecombe about a mile to the north of Patcham. The main road had hitherto passed through the centre of old Patcham village, but, following the boundary change, a by-pass was built to the west.

The oldest surviving section of Patcham can be found close to the junction of the old London Road with Church Hill where there is a picturesque mixture of houses and cottages of brick, flint and render. A number of listed buildings front onto Church Hill which is dominated by All Saints Church. The present building was originally Norman, but much of the exterior, along with the West Tower, was the result of 13th century rebuilding. Sadly much of the external flint work has been covered by an unsightly layer of protective render. The north aisle is late Victorian. In 1880 a painting of the Last Judgement was discovered above the chancel arch. It had lain beneath 30 coats of whitewash and at least two later post-reformation paintings. The fresco, dating from 1230, shows the souls of the dead being weighed before Christ, a subject popular with mediaeval painters. There is a monument to Richard Shelley, a 16th century occupant of

Patcham Place and a forebear of the poet, flanked by a pair of naked grave diggers.

To the north of the church stands the old Tythe barn, 80 metres long, which dates from the 17th century. This has recently been converted into 7 luxury dwellings and a community hall, a development which encountered much local opposition, and which was finally approved by the Secretary of State following a public enquiry. To the east is the 17th century dove-cote of Court Farmhouse, the only scheduled monument in Brighton. It is circular in plan with flint walls and brick buttresses under a conical roof, and originally contained 550 nesting boxes.

13F Patcham, All Saint's Church.

13F Patcham, dove-cote.

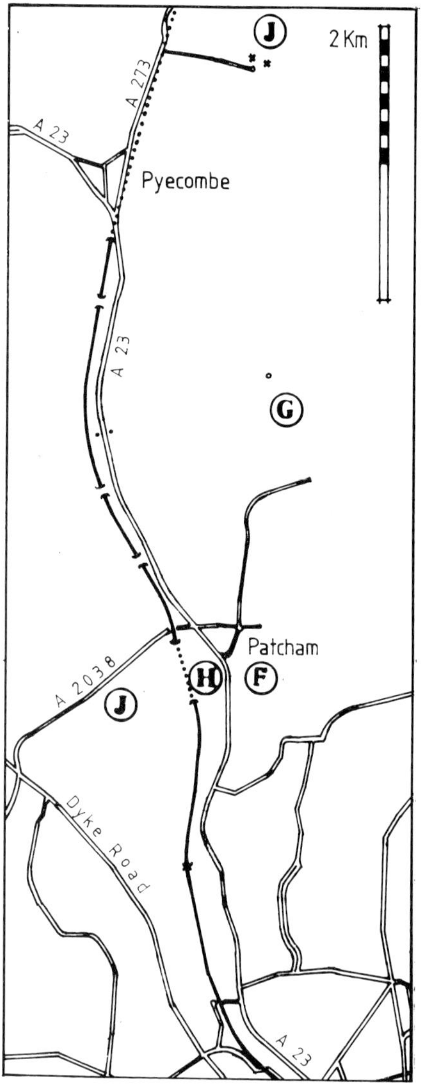

13G The Chattri
Holt Hill, 1 mile north of Patcham

Church Hill terminates at its junction with Brighton's northern ringroad, but a farm track continues northwards up a ridge towards the downs and leads after about a mile to Brighton's strangest and most moving monument. During the First World War the Royal Pavilion was used as a hospital to treat wounded Indian soldiers. Those soldiers who died from their wounds were cremated at a burning ghat on the downs above Patcham. After the war the Indian Government paid for

13G The Chattri.

the building of the Chattri as a memorial to the soldiers who had died fighting a foreigners' war in a foreign land. The memorial was designed by E. C. Henriques, an Indian student studying in London, and takes the form of a simple white marble kiosk in the Moghul style. The Chattri was dedicated in 1921 by the Prince of Wales.

13H Patcham Place
London Road

Patcham Place stands to the west of London Road in an impressive position below a fold in the downs. It has a long history, having been built originally by Sir William West in 1558. A later owner was Richard Shelley, whose monument can be seen in Patcham's Church of All Saints (see 13F). It is sometimes referred to, mistakenly, as an 18th century house, because of its front elevation which resulted from alterations carried out by Squire John Payne in 1764. The north front is an unusual example of the use of black mathematical tiles: these are usually found on terraced town houses in central Brighton. It has seven bays, the centre three projecting under a timber pediment. On the east side

13H Patcham Place.

there are two projecting bay windows. The house and its grounds were acquired by Brighton Corporation in 1937 and now serve as a Youth Hostel.

13J Windmills

Windmills first appeared in England during the 13th century. The downland around Brighton must, at one time, have been studded with them and today a number of well preserved examples remain. Patcham Windmill lies half a mile to the west of the village on the very edge of the connurbation. It was built in 1885 at a cost of £1,400 and was the last working windmill to be put up in Sussex. The original owner was a local baker, Mr. Joseph Hains, who wanted to sell bread baked from home milled wheat. It was used until 1924 when it was sold for £150. Today it has been converted into a private dwelling. Two and a half miles north of Patcham on the northern escarpment of the downs above the village of Clayton there is a pair of windmills known as "Jack and Jill".

13J Clayton Windmills.

Jill is a post mill built in the early 19th century by Henry Lashmar on a site above the Belmont Tunnel. In 1839 it was dragged to its present site by a team of eighty-six oxen. The mill continued to work until 1907, after which date it fell gradually into disrepair. A preservation society has been working since 1979 to restore it and it is hoped that it will soon be in working order again. The original Jack was built in 1765, but it was replaced by the present tower mill with revolving top dome in 1886. The builder, Mr. Cooper from Henfield, used the large brake wheel from the original mill. Jack is much bigger than Jill, having an internal diameter of 4.8 metres under the cap. Jack also stopped work in 1907 and fell into disrepair. New sweeps were added in 1973.

14 HOVE

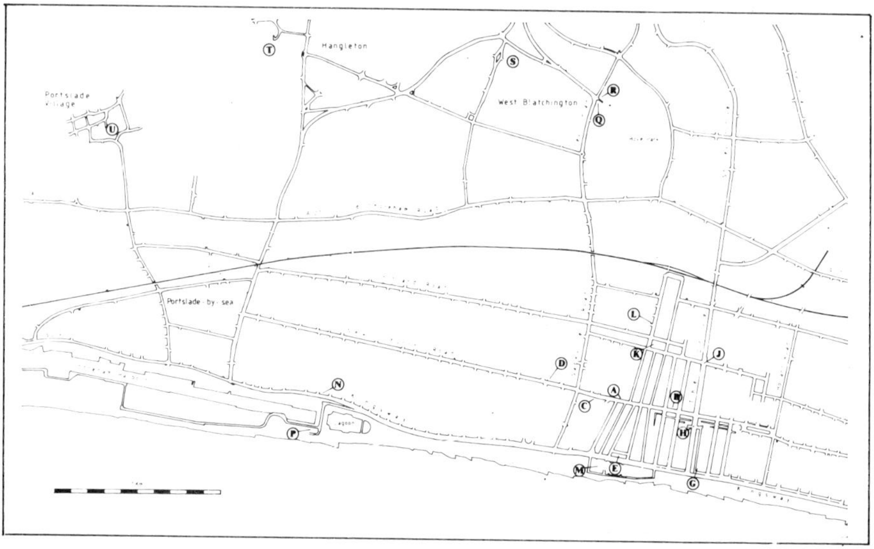

The parish of Hove was transformed from farmland into a somewhat sombre middle class resort town during the 19th century. In 1801 the population stood at about 100 and was concentrated mainly in Hove Village which was situated in the south-west of the parish close to what is now Hove Street. Wick Farm, the home of the Scutt family stood on a hill between Hove and Brighton, and close by, on what is now St. Anne's Well Gardens, a flourishing spa exploited the waters of the Chalybeate Spring. During the 1820s Brunswick Town was developed on land lying just within the south-eastern borders of the parish. This had little effect on the village of Hove and functioned very much as a satellite of Brighton. By 1841 the parish population had increased to 2,500, mainly as a result of the Brunswick development The western expansion of Brighton was now blocked by the Stanford Estate. During the 1850s farmland immediately to the east of Hove Village was sold and the first Victorian villas appeared in a separate suburb known as Cliftonville. Cliftonville had its own railway station, later renamed as Hove Station, and its own shopping centre in George Street. The area south of Church Road and bounded by Osborne Villas and Albany Villas was developed in the early 1850s. Development then moved northwards, Denmark and Goldstone Villas being built after 1860. By 1871 Hove Parish had a population of 11,000, divided between Brunswick Town and Cliftonville, though the two developments were still separated by the farmland of the Stanford Estate. Finally after 1871 the Stanford Estate was opened up for development, though strict covenants ensured that freeholds would only be granted to houses which conformed to the highest building standards. Today the broad avenues of eastern Hove lying on either side of Grand Avenue and the Drive are the result of this period of controlled development. During the next 20 years Hove's population grew to 26,000 and, in spite of various attempts by neighbouring Brighton to annexe the parish within its newly constituted borough boundaries, Hove became an urban district in 1894 and a borough in 1898. After the First World War Hove spread northwards and westwards into Tongdean, Blatchington, and Hangleton. Fine examples of interwar suburban housing can be seen at Tongdean as for instance in Woodland Drive and Tongdean Avenue. Today Hove has very much the character of a large residential suburb, its major social and civic facilities consisting of parks, gardens, tennis courts, bowling greens and churches. Brighton was left with the responsibility for developing the theatres, piers, shops and hotels which were needed to serve Hove's growing resort population.

14A St. Andrew's Church
Church Road

St. Andrew's Church had fallen into a state of decay after the collapse of its main tower during the 16th century. The increase of Hove's population during the early 19th century led to calls for a new church. In 1828 a church was built in Waterloo Street to serve Brunswick Town and functioned as a chapel of ease to St. Andrew's. In 1833 a public meeting was held to determine the future of the old parish church. The architect George Basevi (see 8G) carried out a survey and recommended rebuilding at a cost of £2,000. It was decided to rebuild the church in its original form and Basevi was appointed as the architect. The new building was completed in 1836 and a vestry was added in 1841. The neo-Norman exterior dates entirely from 1836 and only the foundations and some parts of the interior structure remain from the original 12th century building. In 1880 Church Street was extended westwards to create Church Road and a 10 metre strip of the churchyard was lost. The Brighton and Hove Gas Works were established to the immediate east of the churchyard at about the same time. St. Andrew's functioned for many years as Hove's Parish Church but after 1892 this distinction was passed to All Saints in Eaton Road (see 14K).

14A St. Andrew's Church.

14B Hove Town Hall
Norton Road

The Town Hall had been built in Brunswick Street West in 1856 to serve Brunswick Town and, in 1873, this became the temporary home of Hove Town Hall. In 1882 a magnificent new building was opened in Church Road.

14B The Old Town Hall.

The architect was Alfred Waterhouse who was later to design the Metropole Hotel on Brighton's seafront (see 9G). Pevsner described it as red, Gothic, hard and imperishable. Sadly he was wrong on at least one score: the building was destroyed in a fire on New Year's Eve of 1966. The Brighton architects, John Wells-Thorpe and Suppel, were appointed to design a replacement. Work on the new building started in 1970, and the official opening took place in 1974. The new Town Hall cost £2.9 million to build. It contains a concert hall capable of seating 1,400 people, two reception rooms, a council chamber, committee rooms and offices. More than a mere administrative complex, it acts as a focal point for the social and cultural life of the community. Externally the building is a monumental and almost sumptuous reworking of the "beton brut" style of the 1960s. It uses natural finishes, shuttered concrete and exposed aggregate panels, in conjunction with large areas of glazing. Neither the form of the building nor its materials could be described as contextual, and yet it manages through the articulation of plan and elevation to fit well into its surroundings.

14C Hove Public Library
Church Road
Hove's first free library was opened in Grand Avenue in 1891 and moved to Third Avenue in 1901. In 1903 Andrew Carnegie offered £10,000 to help set up a purpose-built library. The site chosen in Church Road was one previously occupied by a Corporation depot. A competition was held and the selected design was by the architects Percy Robinson and W. Alban Jones of Leeds. The new building was opened in 1908. The front facade is in the Edwardian classical revival style, slightly reminiscent of Lutyens and very much of its time. A domed rotunda lights the reference section. Outside and inside are united by a common theme of classical motifs: garlands, scrolls, acorns and oak leaves.

14C Hove Public Library.

14D Hove Museum and Art Gallery
The museum is situated in a freestanding Italianate villa on the corner of Church Road and Pembroke Gardens, and houses an interesting collection of paintings of Hove. A surprising Moghul kiosk adorns the front garden. This is a scaled down model in teak of what would have been a marble garden pavilion. The Maharajah of Jaipur had it made for the Indian and Colonial Exhibition which was held in South Kensington in 1886. Later it was dismantled and eventually found its way to Hove where it was rebuilt in 1926.

14E St. Catherine's Terrace.

14E Cliftonville
This small suburb was developed to the east of Hove Village in the 1850s when the westward expansion of Brighton leapfrogged the Stanford Estate. The area defined by Osborne and Albany Villas contains some delightful mid-Victorian houses. Bonneted bay windows and iron balconies provide a nostalgic Regency flavour in what is essentially a Victorian suburb. The moment of transition can best be seen in St. Catherine's Terrace where the splayed two storey bay windows, the canopies, the balustrades, the decorated timber columns and the tuscan doorways are all of early Victorian design.

14F The Avenues
The land between Brunswick Town and Cliftonville was part of the Stanford Estate, the development of which was blocked during the minority of Ellen Stanford (see 13). When the land was finally released during the 1870s it was planned as the West Brighton Estate, a grid of broad avenues on a grand scale. The subsequent development adopted the heavy monumentality of the later Victorian period. A number of architectural styles appeared as the developers tried to come up with a commercially viable formula: yellow brick Italianate in First and Second Avenues, red brick Queen Anne revival in parts of Grand Avenue. The area is rich in ornate balconies,

14D Hove Museum and Art Gallery.

decorated brickwork and terracotta reliefs. The main avenues run from north to south terminating with a view of the sea at Kingsway. At the northern end a series of delightful mews have been tucked in behind the fronts of Church Road. These served originally as stables for the adjoining mansions. Today, quite appropriately, they are used as back street repair garages. King's Mews off Third Avenue is a delightful composition of yellow brick hidden behind a pair of monumental lodges.

14F Kings Mews.

14G South Eastern Electricity Headquarters
Grand Avenue

The SEEBoard Building was built originally in 1874 as Princes' Hotel to designs by Sir James Knowles. The building employed yellow brickwork and was in an Italiante style sometimes referred to as Tuscan. It occupied a commanding position on the southeast corner of Grand Avenue enjoying views across the Kingsway towards the sea. Knowles was also responsible for much of the housing in the immediate area, and is better known as the architect of London's Grosvenor Hotel. The hotel prospered and during the 1930s it expanded northwards along Grand Avenue. It was used by the Royal Navy during the war and in 1949 it was sold to the Electricity Board. The main building was refurbished in 1981 and a new northern extension, designed by the Miller Bourne Partnership, was added sympathetically to the north.

14G West Brighton Estate as projected by Knowles c.1870.

14H St. George's Memorial
Grand Avenue

St. George's Memorial stands in the middle of Grand Avenue and offers an elegant and restrained homage to the citizens of Hove who died during the First World War. It was designed by Sir Edwin Lutyens and consists of a bronze statue of St. George on a simple column and pedestal of granite.

14H St. George's Memorial.

14J The Drive

The northern extension of Grand Avenue was developed during the last two decades of the 19th century. Here the buildings reflect the confidence, the affluence and bizarre tastes of their period. H. B. Measures, a London architect who had been responsible for part of the residential area behind Harrods in London's Knightsbridge, designed nos. 69-79, The Drive for William Willett in 1887. These are large mansion houses in red brick with terracotta detailing, and show an almost neurotic variation of roof level, gable design, and facade decoration. The area is rich in decorative details: terracotta dragons guard scrolled and pedimented gables, pepperpot turrets pop out from eaves and extravagant porches advance towards the pavement.

14J Pedimented Gable with Dragons.

14K The Church of All Saints
Eaton Road

The Church of All Saints was designed in 1889 by J. L. Pearson, the architect of Truro Cathedral, and in 1892 was designated as Hove's Parish Church. Pearson had already completed the ornate Tudor vicarage in 1883 when he was commissioned by Cannon Thomas Peacey to design the church itself. The style is a pure 13th century Gothic delivered in yellow Sussex sandstone, now much discoloured. The design was ambitious and the scale of the interior is massive. Building progress was slow and the chancel and sanctuary were not completed until 1901. Pearson had planned a tower and spire in keeping with the rest of the design, but the project ran out of funds in 1908 and the tower remains an unfinished stump to this day.

14K The Church of All Saints.

14L Europa House
Goldstone Villas

A redundant non-conformist chapel, built originally in 1878, has been skilfully converted into offices for Olivetti by the London architects Edward Cullinan and Partners. The building was sold in 1968 for £12,000 and the renovations of the early 1970s cost £33,000. The stuccoed shell of this neo-classical building consists of five bays with Tuscan pilasters, a front pediment, arched first floor windows and a rusticated piano nobile. All of this has been kept and a thoroughly modern office building has been cleverly inserted within it. The main timber floor was retained and a new upper floor of concrete was installed with support from columns which bear on new basement footings. A splayed staircase of steel and slate rises from the pavement to the main entry level. A central double height corridor crosses the building from the main entrance to link with a glass staircase which breaks out of the rear elevation.

14L Europa House.

14M The King Alfred Sports Centre
Kingsway

The old King Alfred Baths were built in 1938 and came to be known as the Hove Marina. The building was taken over by the Admiralty during the War and renamed HMS King Alfred. In 1946 it reopened to the public and was rechristened the King Alfred Swimming Pool. The building was expensive to maintain and the concrete structure needed to be strengthened. During the 1970s expensive repairs were carried out to the main plunge pool. Finally in 1980 the buildings were remodelled and a new extension was built on the sea-side to designs by Scott, Brownrigg and Turner. The new centre opened in 1982, having cost £3.7 million to build. It has a tubular steel roof supporting polycarbonate glazing above a precast concrete and brick structure. The interior is finished with glazed tiles and is said to create a pier-like atmosphere.

14N Caffyn's Garage — The Motor Depot
Kingsway

This garage was designed in the late 1920s by the architect E. J. Love, and was built by the Worthing Estates Building Company. It is similar in style to Shoreham Airport (see 18F), though its moderne image recalls the work of Oliver Hill and E. B. Musman. The front building contains an entrance foyer, a reception and a showroom with offices at first floor. It is no more than 5 metres deep and acts as a screen to a more conventional set of brick workshops to the rear.

Originally faced with faience tiles it has been heavily coated in white paint and now appears from a distance to be rendered. Such buildings celebrated the wonders of the new age of the motor car and offered a popular reworking of expressionist forms. Pevsner and other modern movement historians were wont to dismiss this sort of building as being without value, but Caffyn's Garage stands as an elegant memorial to the ideas and aspirations of another age.

14P Hove Seaside Villas.

14P Hove Seaside Villas
Western Esplanade

These seaside villas were built in 1910 and designed by the architect E. J. Holland. They were constructed from concrete block and have rusticated bases and machicolated parapets. The ground floors are raised nearly 2 metres above road level and the entrances are reached via a flight of steps through an opening in the 3 metre high wall. It is thought that the castellated appearance was inspired by contemporary lighthouse structures and by similarly machicolated Edwardian country houses.

14N Caffyn's Garage — The Motor Depot.

14Q The Co-Op Superstore

The Co-Op Superstore was completed in 1986 having been built in less than one year. The store was designed by the Elsworth Sykes Partnership in conjunction with the Co-operative Wholesale Society's Property Group. The second of a number of out-of-town hypermarkets which have been projected for the periphery of the conurbation, the store provides a one stop shopping facility within a large car park. The vast sales hall is disguised by elevations of brick and tile which take their inspiration in part from the surrounding suburbs and in part from the nearby Engineerium. The architects have worked with skill and care to meet their clients' requirements for a massive development and have avoided damaging a sensitive suburban context. Like the Engineerium and the similar Sainsbury's Store in Lewes Road (see 12) the Co-op building has been designed to turn a utilitarian shed into something which it is not. There is no doubt that this approach is popular with the public and meets the requirements of the planners, but it is also indicative of the massive loss of nerve which currently afflicts the architectural profession.

14Q The Co-Op Superstore.

14R The British Engineerium Nevill Road

The rapid growth of Brighton during the 19th century placed great strains on the existing water supply system. A new pumping station was needed and in 1866 a site was chosen at Goldstone Bottom, a depression in the downs. By 1875 two enormous beam engines were drawing millions of gallons of water each day from wells which connected to a system of fissures in the chalk of the Downs. The pumping station continued to function until the early 1950s after which the buildings and their machinery were allowed to fall into disrepair. Finally the Department of the Environment placed a preservation order on the buildings and in 1974 Jonathan Minns was granted a lease which made it possible for him to set up the British Engineerium Trust: his aim was to restore both the buildings and the machinery and to establish a museum of engineering. After 2 years of hard work the museum opened in 1976. The coal store now serves an exhibition hall and contains the Corliss engine which had been shown at the 1889 Paris Exhibition. The engine houses and the main chimney have been carefully restored and now stand as fine examples of Victorian industrial architecture with heavily decorated polychrome brickwork. The main beam engines are now in beautiful condition and reveal the extent to which Victorian engineers decorated even the most utilitarian of objects with rich pseudo classical details.

14S West Blatchington

Nevill Road leads out of Hove to West Blatchington, once a downland village but now totally submerged by postwar suburban development. The Church of St. Peter was built originally in 1890 but much of what is seen today is the result of sensitive rebuilding carried out by John Leopold Denman (see 1J) in 1961.

To the south lies Blatchington Mill, a hexagonal smock mill of a type commonly built during the 17th century. The building's date is not known, but its existence on November 5th 1825 is recorded in a water colour by John Constable. Smock mills differ from post mills in that the cap and the central wind shaft are the only parts to turn with the wind while the main body and the machinery remain static. The Blatchington mill is set on top of a barn and may have been used to run other farm equipment. The mill was last worked in 1907 and was purchased in 1937 by Hove Corporation for £3,400. It has been extensively restored and is now protected as a listed building.

14S West Blatchington Mill.

14T Hangleton Village

Another downland village drowned in a sea of suburban semis, Hangleton was a thriving community at the time of Domesday, though it was hard hit by the Black Death and was little more than a farming hamlet at the end of the last century. A rather bare green separates St. Helen's Church from the cluster of buildings associated with Hangleton Manor. The church dates back to the 11th century and must therefore be the oldest surviving building in Brighton. The square tower is flint with stone dressings and is 13th century, the nave walls and narrow lancet windows date back to the Conquest. Hangleton Manor is now a pub, but it was the centre of a busy farmyard until the beginning of the present century. The main building was built in 1540 using some stones taken from Lewes Priory (17E). The walls are again flint with stone dressings and the finely carved windows are divided by stone mullions into four and five bays. The interior is marred by various modern additions but in the lounge bar there is 17th century panelling with carved Corinthian pilasters and lengthy inscriptions. The separate building to the north contained stables and servants' quarters and is now a private house. South of the Manor House is a ruined dovecote with flint walls and chalk nesting boxes. This interesting structure is being carefully restored by a group of local volunteers.

14U Portslade Village

The third of the trio of downland villages swallowed up by Hove's low density sprawl, Portslade is now something of jumble lost behind a labyrinth of enormous flint walls. The church of St. Nicholas dates from the 12th and 13th century with Victorian additions and has an interesting crenellated tower. East of the church is St. Mary's Convent which stands in the grounds of the now ruined Portslade Manor. South of the church on Locks Hill is the Lodge, an attractive Regency Villa built in 1786 and looking slightly out of place. The "Le Carbone" factory, originally a Victorian brewery, dominates the narrow High Street. Its astonishing five storeys of yellow brickwork are decorated with arches and dentels and stuccoed string courses. The immense chimney, dwarfing the tiny village lane, springs from a decorative stuccoed base which advertises 1881 as the year of its construction.

15 ROTTINGDEAN & SALTDEAN

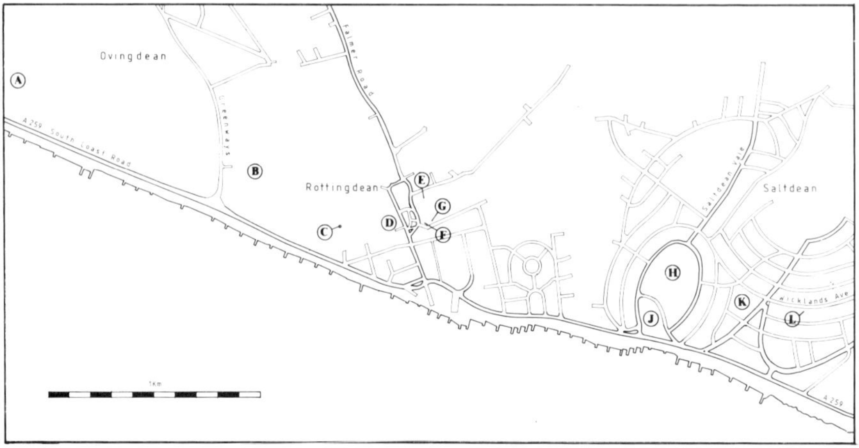

Rottingdean and Saltdean mark the eastern edge of the Brighton conurbation and were incorporated within the borough at the time of the 1928 boundary changes. Rottingdean is an old fishing and farming village occupying a dip in the downs which corresponds to a break in the cliffs. Today, in spite of being in reality a residential suburb with resort appendages, it still retains a certain traditional charm. Its neighbour Saltdean, on the other hand, is very much a product of the interwar years and now exudes a slightly old-fashioned modernity.

15A Roedean School

During the 19th century many private schools were established in Brighton. Two sisters, the Misses Lawrence, founded a girls' school in Lewes Crescent in 1885. Later they purchased 7 hectares of land on the cliffs between Brighton and Rottingdean from the Marquess of Abergavenny with a view to erecting "a really suitable school building in which the school can have a permanent existence". Thus England's most famous and most exclusive girls' public school was born. The sisters employed John W. Simpson as their architect and the new school opened in 1899. The buildings stand aloof on the edge of the downs, with little in the way of landscape to soften their profiles. The style has been described as "free Jacobean" and there is a strange superimposition of Arts and Crafts detailing upon a strict and formal plan. In the original composition all the main elements of the school were united under one roof with the shared elements occupying a middle section and the four 'houses' occupying the wings. A chapel was added in 1906 and a Library and Art School in 1911. The detached block to the north east contains the Junior School and the Sanatorium.

15A Roedean School.

15B Saint Dunstan's
St. Dunstan's is a residential unit catering for the rehabilitation of blinded servicemen. It was designed by Sir John Burnet, Tait and Lorne and built between 1937 and 1939. The style is International Modern but has more in common with the Dutch School or with Holden's London Underground stations than with Mendelsohn's Bexhill pavilion. The building has a symmetrical plan set monumentally against the hillside. The verticality of the composition contrasts with the horizontality of the bands of brickwork and glazing, the net effect falling somewhere between suburban signal box and coastguard station. The plan form resembles that of a biplane to which the residents could easily relate.

15B St. Dunstan's.

15C Rottingdean Windmill
Beacon Hill, Rottingdean
The black-tarred smock mill on Beacon Hill dates from the 18th century. It originally occupied a site close to the present cricket field and was dragged to its present position by a team of oxen in 1802. The artist William Nicholson, who was living in the Grange at Rottingdean, used it in 1897 as the basis of his design for a logo for the publishers William Heinemann and Sons. The mill was repaired in 1935 by Brighton Corporation and is now looked after by the Rottingdean Preservation Society with help from Heinemann.

15D Rottingdean Village
The village of Rottingdean can be traced back to Saxon times. Its name meant originally the "valley of Rota's people". The main part of the village nestles in the bottom of a protective valley and seems remote from either the coast or the busy A259, both of which lie only a few hundred yards away to the south. Rottingdean grew during the 19th century as a small resort, very much in the wake of Brighton and at one time they were connected by Magnus Volk's bizarre marine railway. At times there was a strong risk that the village would suffer the same fate as Woodingdean two miles to the north and be swalled up in modern housing developments. However, in 1928 Rottingdean was included within the expanded boundaries of Brighton, a fact which helped to limit development, and it remains one of the most charming of the town's satellite villages.

15E St. Margaret's Church.

15E St. Margaret's Church
Rottingdean

A stone church is known to have stood on this site in the days before the Norman Conquest, and its foundations are incorporated within the present buildings. The nave and parts of the south transept are Norman, but much of the rest is Early English. The church has flint walls and a dominant central tower, built to replace the original 12th century tower after its destruction during a gale. Further rebuilding took place during the late 14th century following damage inflicted by French raiders. Finally in 1856 considerable restoration was carried out by Sir Giles Gilbert Scott. There is interesting stained glass, some of it by Burne-Jones who lived for a time in the village and is buried in the churchyard, and some by Morris and Co.

15F The Grange
Rottingdean Village

It is said that in 1355 the Black Prince stayed in the house which previously occupied this site, and that his ghost occasionally makes a return visit. The present house was built originally in 1792 by Dr. Hooker to serve as vicarage to St. Margaret's Church and has a Georgian front of seven bays. It was renamed "The Grange" by Sir William Nicholson, the painter, who lived in it from 1908 to 1914. In 1919 Sir Edwin Lutyens remodelled the

15F The Grange, front.

interiors for Sir George Lewis, adding a new rear elevation and elaborate painted wooden floor tiling. A garden studio was also added at this time. The building now houses Rottingdean's Public Library and Museum. A mulberry tree in the garden is thought to be one of the earliest in the country, having been planted during the reign of James I as part of an attempt to produce silk.

15F The Grange, rear.

15G The Whiteway Centre.

15G The Whiteway Centre
Rottingdean Village

The Whiteway Centre was designed by the Lewes based firm of Michael Blee and Partners and was built in 1974. It functions as a community centre for the village and complements the activities of the school, the library and the two village churches. The site was originally part of the garden of the Grange, and lies within the village conservation area. The buildings sit between the Grange and the small studio which Lutyens built for Nicholson and which for some time had been used as a guide hut. The centre itself occupies three sides of an open courtyard which is completed on the fourth side by the studio. The three main elements, hall, youth club and committee room, are linked by a spine of ancillary rooms which are built onto an old garden wall. The massing is consciously picturesque and creates the effect of a group of farm buildings.

The materials, flint, brick, clay tiles and horizontal boarding, relate well to neighbouring buildings and to the village and yet the design avoids pastiche and is surprisingly modern in spirit.

15J The Lido.

15H Saltdean

Saltdean is an eastern extension of Rottingdean occupying the next dip in the cliffs. Much of it was developed during the 1920s at a time when there was a high demand for retirement and holiday homes on sites along the south coast. Developers had access to cheap land, interest rates were low, and planning restrictions almost non-existent. The Lido and the Ocean Hotel have left Saltdean with an image of seaside modern: the invasion of white international style architecture from the continent during the 1930s failed to penetrate very much further than the beaches of the south coast!

15J The Lido
Saltdean

The Saltdean Lido was designed in 1938 by R. W. H. Jones. Jones was obviously influenced by the work of Eric Mendelsohn, and in particular by his designs for the De La Warr Pavilion in Bexhill. This can be seen in the use of curvilinear forms for the walls and the glazing, and in the stream-lined handrails. The plan organisation owes something to contemporary buildings such as the Finsbury Health Centre by Lubetkin. This is a building which shows clearly the enormous influence exerted by European immigrant architects during the 1930s and the combination of white International Modern styling with Beaux Arts planning went on to become almost the hallmark of English seaside architecture. The building is laid out symmetrically with a central two storey block containing the main entrance foyer with its obligatory spiral staircases leading to the cafe and sun deck and two single storey curved wings containing the main dressing rooms. The swimming pool is protected by the projecting wings and can accommodate 500 bathers. Sadly the original three-tiered reinforced concrete diving board which originally echoed the lines of the main building and formed an essential element of the composition no longer exists.

15J The Lido.

15K The Ocean Hotel
Lagrange Avenue, Saltdean

15K Ocean Hotel Inland Entrance.

R. W. H. Jones also built the Ocean Hotel in 1938. The buildings occupy a hillside overlooking the valley and the seashore and are oriented towards the southwest. The site is fan-shaped and slopes over 15 metres from back to front. This was no ordinary hotel, but rather a sort of budget priced hydro developed to bring seaside holidays within a price which could be afforded by working class families from the cities. The central facilities of the hotel were arranged on the main axis with the six "dormitory blocks" stepping down the slope on either side. The composition cleverly contrived to create a series of sun terraces at each level which met finally at a swimming pool which straddles the axis. Sadly some of the terraces have been enclosed and the pool is covered by what can only be described as a factory shed. In spite of its modern design, the building now has an old-fashioned atmosphere and seems to be a relic from far-off days before package tours to Spain were ever dreamt of.

15K Ocean Hotel.

15L Houses by Connell, Ward and Lucas
Wicklands Avenue

The firm of Connell, Ward and Lucas was founded in the late 1920s by a young New Zealander called Amyas Connell and was responsible for some of the earliest examples of modern cubist architecture in Britain. In 1934 they built three private houses at Saltdean on the hillside overlooking the sea. These were part of what was intended to be a much larger demonstration project which would show off the new aesthetic. Although only three houses were built, a number of later houses in Saltdean seem to have been influenced by them. Indeed when the later work of R. W. H. Jones is considered, Saltdean seems to have been a centre on the south coast for the international modern style. Today only two of the original trio survive, and these have been so much altered as to be almost unrecognisable: they look more like comfortable suburban homes than iconoclast machines for living.

15L One of the houses.

16 STANMER

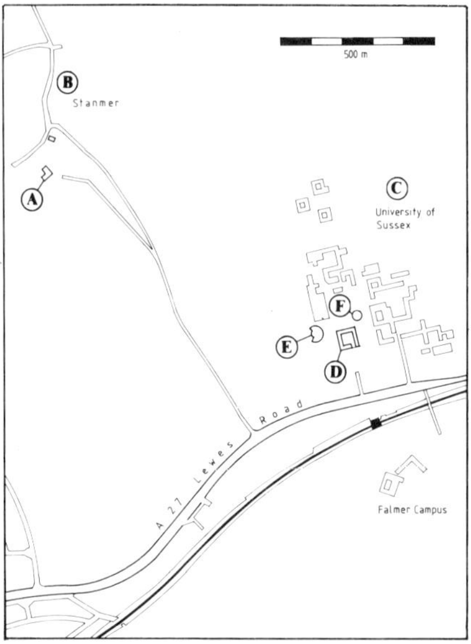

The name "Stanmer" is derived from the Anglo-Saxon words, "staen" and "mere", which together mean "the pool of stones", a reference to the "greywethers", a circle of stones which surround the pond beside Stanmer Church. The land forming the nucleus of the present estate was purchased in 1713 by Henry Pelham of Lewes, a local landowner. Successive generations of Pelhams systematically built up the estate by purchasing surrounding farms, until by 1840, it had become the largest downland holding to the east of Brighton. After 1880, however, the Pelhams failed to keep abreast of new developments in farming and the estate went into a decline which led to the piecemeal sale of land. During the Second World War the much depleted estate of 2,000 hectares was used as a battle training ground and in 1947 it was finally sold to Brighton Corporation, thus saving its delightful park from the developer's bulldozer. Sussex University now occupies 80 hectares of the estate, the rest being preserved as farmland and public park.

16A Stanmer House

Henry Pelham died in 1721, eight years after acquiring the Stanmer Estate. He was succeeded by his son, Henry Pelham Junior, who resolved to rebuild the existing family house. His chosen architect for this undertaking was Nicholas Dubois, the translator of Leoni's English edition of Palladio's "Four Books". Not surprisingly, Dubois produced a Palladian design. Stanmer House is his only surviving building in England. Henry Pelham Junior died during building and his brother Thomas completed the house in 1727 at a cost of £14,000.

The main elevation, which faces east, is of fine ashlar and has eight bays of which three project under a pediment. The cornice and the rusticated porch are later additions. The north wing is built of brick and flint and originally contained servants' quarters. The interiors were badly damaged during the wartime occupation, but fine 18th century plaster ceilings remain in the dining room and the drawing room. The entrance hall has niches for displaying busts and a simple stone fireplace surmounted by the Pelham Arms. Rising out of the hall is an oak staircase with Corinthian balusters which was built by a Lewes carpenter for the sum of £20.

16A Stanmer House.

16B Stanmer Village

The present village church was built in 1838 by Henry Pelham, 6th Earl of Chichester, to replace an earlier church which had been destroyed by fire in 1837. It is built of flint and has a slender west tower under a shingled roof. Monuments to Pelham ancestors were moved here from the London Church of the Holy Trinity, Minories, when it was demolished.

Stanmer Village lies to the north of the church and contains a number of 18th and 19th century buildings. These include a traditional 'long barn' with three flint elevations and one of weather boarding under an interesting hipped roof which is supported on tie beams, braces and queen posts.

16C Falmer House, University of Sussex.

16C The University of Sussex

Sussex University was the first of seven new universities which were built during the 1960s. It opened in temporary accommodation near Preston Park with 50 students in 1961. The idea for a university in Brighton had first been proposed by Charles Clayton, a local architect, at a public meeting in 1911 and was revived in 1956 by William Stone, Brighton's Director of Education. The government was about to embark on a university building programme in order both to extend the availability of higher education and to accommodate the post war birth bulge. Official approval for a new university in Brighton was given by the University Grants Commission in 1958. In 1959 the architect Basil Spence was commissioned to prepare a master plan for the new campus, as well as detailed designs for the first building phase. The campus occupies 80 hectares of Stanmer Park and is situated 4 miles from Brighton in a beautiful 18th century parkland setting. It occupies a valley which slopes gently northwards from the main road linking Brighton to Lewes. Spence's master plan is a direct response to the topography and landscape of the site. A minimum number of trees were felled and the valley generates the main axis of the buildings and the main thrust of the circulation. The buildings are generally low and create between them open courts and terraces which exploit views to the park beyond. The design is a fusion of the Oxbridge quadrangle principle with modern forms derived from le Corbusier's Maison Jaoul and employs traditional Sussex building materials. In the early buildings Spence established a vocabulary of arches and vaults in concrete and massive piers in soft red brick. The need to economise led to the simplifcation of this vocabulary during later phases.

Student residences were not included in the early phases, and it was thought that the student population could be dove-tailed into Brighton's holiday guest houses during the off-season. Later a number of hostel schemes were built in the northern part of the campus, notably by the architects Maguire and Murray, and Hughes, Lomax and Adutt.

16D Falmer House — University of Sussex

Falmer House was part of the first phase of building and with it Basil Spence established the campus vocabulary of concrete arches and vaults with piers of red brick. It acts as a monumental gatehouse, straddling the main axis of the campus, and is entered under a massive 11 metre high vault. Huge voids frame views of the landscape and seem to suggest missing rooms while the central quadrangle floats on a limpid moat. It forms the social heart of the University and originally contained refectories, the Students' Union and the Senior Common Room. The construction work was programmed to be completed within a 21 month period and the consulting engineers, Ove Arup and Partners, developed a special system of pre-fabricated beams in an effort to meet the deadline. For the same reason self-finishing materials were specified for the interiors. The design offers echoes of Piranesi and le Corbusier and it was greeted as a major building, receiving an RIBA award in 1964. In 1966 the refectories were moved to another location.

16D Falmer House.

16E The Gardner Arts Centre — University of Sussex

The arts centre was founded in 1962 with the aim of strengthening ties with the local community, as well as creating a focal point for the cultural life of the University. Funds came from the Gulbenkian Foundation and from Dr. Lydden Gardner, after whom the centre was eventually named. Sadly Dr. Gardner died before the building was completed in 1969. The building was designed by Sir Basil Spence, Bonnington and Collins in association with Sean Kenny the well-known theatre consultant. The circular auditorium was planned to seat up to 600 people in a number of different configurations of stage and audience. Initially it was possible to create an open stage, a proscenium stage, arena staging and a juxtaposition of multiple stages. However, the process of transformation proved too costly and cumbersome and the auditorium was later altered to provide a more conventional seating arrangement. The theatre itself is surrounded by a complex of circular drums which house the stage facilities, the foyer and bars, an exhibition gallery, practice rooms for music and studios for painting and pottery. These elements intercommunicate in such a way as to bring together the various branches of the arts. The architects intended the area between the building and the side of the valley to be used as an open-air theatre, but the rake of the ground is too steep and it has apparently never been used.

16F The Meeting House — University of Sussex

Soon after the founding of the University, Alderman Caffyn, the Chairman of the University Council, offered to build an Anglican chapel on the campus. This offer was rejected by students and staff as being too sectarian, and an alternative proposal to build several smaller chapels of different

16F The Meeting House.

denominations was canvassed. Finally the matter was resolved by Lady Fulton, the wife of the University's first Principal, who proposed the building of a non-denominational "Meeting House".

The Meeting House was very much the personal design of Sir Basil Spence, and he placed it close to the main axis of the campus between the Physics Building and Falmer House. His first design was for a circular building with a conical roof reminiscent of a traditional oast house. In spite of the fact that the architect had by this time been knighted and had received numerous awards for his buildings, his design was turned down by the Brighton Planning Committee! A second, simpler design was later approved. It has a circular plan with walls built from honeycombed blockwork with pieces of coloured glass inserted within the voids.

16 University of Sussex.

17 LEWES

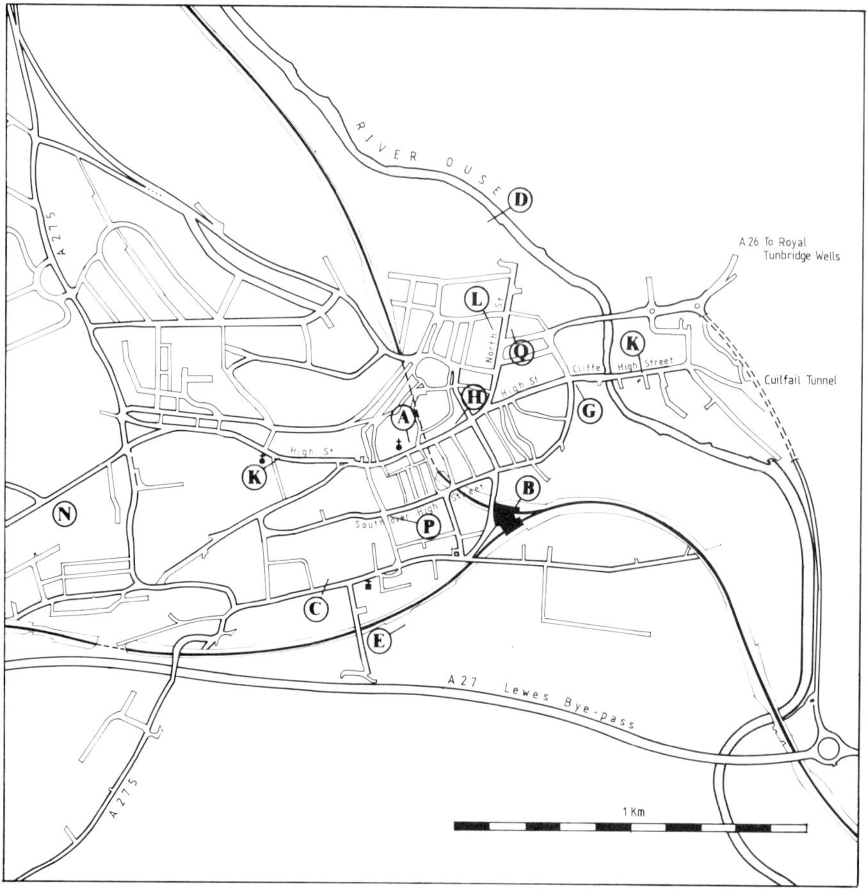

Lewes was a Saxon town which, as a result of its commercial, administrative and strategic importance, became the County Town of East Sussex. This was largely due to its location on a navigable river and a defendable hill. It lies on the boundary between two agricultural regions offering a wide variety of products for marketing within the area and for export. From the Norman Conquest it was a transit point for much commercial traffic either crossing the River Ouse or disembarking there from ships. For most of the 19th century it was a prominent market town with a considerable industrial base, but from the late 19th century, rail transport and the growth of the port of Newhaven eroded Lewes's role as a port and as a regional market centre. Lewes's emphasis is now towards tourism and the administration of the county.

The futures of Brighton and Lewes became interlinked during the late 18th century. Lewes was the birthplace or original workplace of some of Brighton's influential personalities. It was also the source of some of Brighton's constructional techniques.

Dr. Russell, a Lewes resident, prescribed the seaside air as a cure for his patients from the environs of Lewes and helped to initiate the building of the Brighton resort around the decaying seafaring town. Thomas Read Kemp, Member of Parliament in the town, lost large sums of money attempting to create Kemp Town. The Wilds, Amon Wilds and his son Amon Henry Wilds, ran a design and constructional firm in Lewes and were involved in projects like Castle Place, Bartholomew House and the rebuilding of the nave of All Saints, in Friar's Walk. In 1815

17 The Castle from Southover.

the Wilds moved to Brighton where they designed, with Charles Busby, many outstanding examples of Georgian architecture.

Brighton is lacking in examples of buildings constructed before 1700 due to redevelopment during and after the Georgian period. Lewes has many mediaeval buildings and it has fine examples of knapped, squared and coursed flintwork so commonly used in the area after the Norman Conquest. There are a large number of timber framed buildings clad with mathematical tiles. The latter were used in Brighton, but generally on new buildings.

Flintwork facades from several centuries survive in Lewes, becoming increasingly refined as they progress into the Georgian period and also more geometric and labour intensive. The flintwork in Brighton is of the 18th and 19th centuries only. Flints are found in quantity in chalk and were known by the Neolithic inhabitants as an extremely hard stone suitable for shaping into tools.

The earliest examples of flint used in a rough fashion are to be seen in the Priory of St. Pancras and in the Castle Keep. During the 14th century flint came to be used often as a durable finish to major buildings and it can be seen broken in half and knapped on the Barbican.

By the 1700s workmanship had progressed to the point where flints could be knapped, coursed and even squared as can be seen on the 1748 elevation of St. Michael's Church. As it was always an expensive method of building, being highly labour intensive, most dwellings were timber framed like the 15th Century Bookshop in the Upper High Street.

Lewes has a total of 60 dwellings clad in mathematical tiles. They were common after 1740 and were used on timber framed buildings to disguise them as solid brick structures. The face of the tile which resembles a brick header is bedded in a lime putty and nailed through a hidden upper portion on to horizontal boards. On a window bay the boards are set vertically. There were problems at the corners where timber quoins were painted to resemble stone and at lintols where a run of headers would be impossible in brick. After 1780 a lead based mix was used to give a black glazed finish to the tiles. This was followed by the manufacture of a popular red tile and later by a "white" tile which was in fact a yellow colour. General use of these tiles was on the wane after 1850, but they continued to be manufactured until 1960 at Burgess Hill where they can still be obtained by special order. They were used in Brighton in several locations, including the Pump House in Market Street (see 2D) and Royal Crescent (see 7E).

17 The Castle drawing by Pauline Sutton.

17A Lewes Castle Keep.

17A Lewes Castle and Barbican
High Street

Lewes developed as a stronghold due to the spur of chalk which offered a fortifiable and commanding position over the first major crossing point of the River Ouse. It was from Roman times an important link in the chain of trade routes through the once marshy areas of Sussex. The Roman road linking London to Malling can still be traced and there is evidence to suggest that an obscure Roman station called "Mutuantonis" was positioned in what is now St. John's Churchyard.

After the Norman Conquest masonry fortification began to be constructed on existing earthworks. William the Conqueror bestowed the "Rape and Town of Lewes" on one of his most powerful barons, and son-in-law, William de Warenne. William built his fortress on the semi-artificial earthworks of two moated mounds. On the southernmost motte he constructed his keep, but according to Pevsner he had an additional keep on Brack Mount. This main shell-keep was built of local flints and it is evident that the flintwork is not of the level of sophistication of that used on the polygonal turrets and the barbican. This is because the turrets are a 13th century addition, while the barbican was completed early in the 14th century and even has squared flints and herringbone coursing.

The castle served largely as a refuge from intermittent attacks by the French. It was barely utilised in the Battle of Lewes which was fought on the South Downs in 1264. The building was vandalised and allowed to become ruinous after the death of the last of the de Warennes in 1347. In the late 18th century the keep was used as a gazebo by the Kemp family during the height of their political and social prominence. Its dominant form is still an arresting landmark in the townscape and it offers excellent views of the river plain and town.

The adjacent Lewes Living History Pavilion describes the town's history in an audio-visual display above a detailed model of the town in the 1880s.

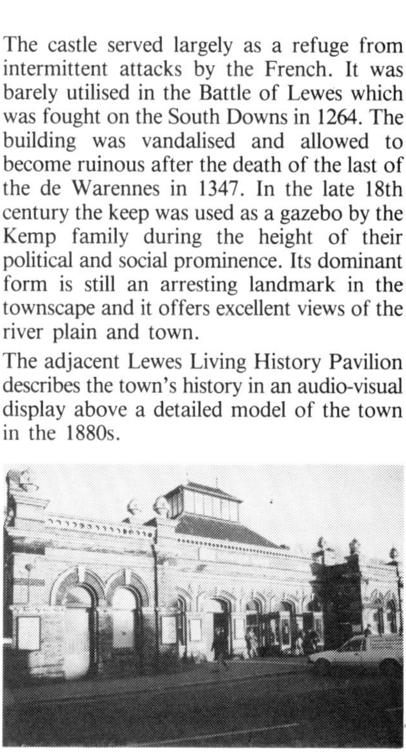

17B The Railway Station.

17A The Barbican.

17B Lewes Railway Station
Station Road

Following the opening of the London to Brighton railway in 1841, proposals were put forward for a line through to Lewes. This was carried out in 1845 when a line was cut through the ruins of the Priory and ended at a terminus station. The Friars Walk station was opened in 1846. Shortly after, the Eastbourne and Hastings line was completed and the Lewes terminus was made redundant.

Forty years later renewed activity by the London, Brighton and South Coast Railway Co. in Sussex led to the construction of many new lines, including a much needed link from Lewes to London and East Grinstead which was opened in 1882. Rerouting of lines resulted in the construction of a tunnel under the castle, the closing of lines on the east side of the town, and the need for a new station. This was to be the third station to be built and was constructed on the triangular area formed by the inter-section of the London to Eastbourne and Brighton to Eastbourne lines.

The architect for the stations on the new lines built in the 1880s appears to have been T. H. Myers of Preston, Lancashire. His free style was warmly received, as a departure from the neo-classical style adopted in the 1840s for the earlier stations in Lewes. Myers's choice of the Queen Anne style of R. Norman Shaw produced station buildings whose main entrance elevations bear reference to the small English country house of the early Renaissance. They incorporate warm colours, red brickwork, timber beams and varied roof forms and building forms. Above this spans the contemporary innovative wrought iron, cast iron and glass roofs, which gives a feeling of space and light lacking in earlier stations.

17C Anne of Cleves' House
Southover High Street

This is a much altered Wealden type house, whose front dates from the early 16th century, and rear from the Elizabethan period. It was never actually visited by Anne of Cleves, Henry VIII's fourth wife, but is nevertheless on the manorial lands given to her by the King. Probably its most interesting feature is the barrel-vaulted cellar under the hall; however, the signs of continuous alteration on the timber structure throughout the house gives a fascinating insight into its history. In the early part of this century much of the building was restored by Walter Godfrey, who was greatly respected for his work in this field. He chose, however, to add windows to the main bedroom and shore up the structure rather than effect a proper restoration. Despite this, the house and museum which is open to the public is worth a prolonged visit.

17D The East Sussex Fire Brigade
Communications Headquarters
North Street

This is the first modern building on the old wharf to acknowledge fully the River Ouse from which sprang much of Lewes's authority. Since the demise of the port of Lewes new buildings have turned their backs to the river. Here the architect, Kate Mackintosh, of the County Architect's Department, has arranged the accommodation in order to give users the full benefit of views of the river.

The building is a computer centre and was completed in July 1985. It was designed to cope with the communications requirements of the Brigade throughout East Sussex. This site was chosen as it gives a clear radio beam to the Police Headquarters's aerial over the river in Malling. The area is liable to flooding and so the service floor was raised 150 mm above the highest recorded flood level. Car parking is located beneath.

The brief called for an unusually flexible servicing arrangement to accommodate future changes in computing and electronic servicing requirements. The design is therefore aimed towards a fully integrated and intelligent high technology building which clearly has prompted the unashamed use of modern materials internally and externally.

17E Priory of St. Pancras 1077-1538
Cockshut Road

This great Cluniac Priory was founded by William de Warenne (see 17A). He and his wife Gundreda had been deeply impressed by the Burgundian Monastery of Cluny and persuaded the Abbot to establish the Priory of St. Pancras, the only Cluniac House in England.

The buildings dominated the river valley for over 450 years, acting as a local cultural and spiritual centre. It provided employment, education and health care, but did not participate in national and political affairs. Its only moment of national significance was when it was handed over to Simon de Montfort by Henry III after his defeat at the Battle of Lewes in 1264.

The Precinct enclosed thirty acres of land and buildings. The most important of these was the Priory Church which was 430ft. in length, longer than Chichester Cathedral. It was modelled on the great Abbey of Cluny in Burgundy and built of Sussex marble. Other buildings included the Infirmary Chapel, believed to have been constructed on the site of a pre-Conquest Saxon church, the Almonry, the Pigeon House for 4,000 birds, the Frater (Refectory), the Dorter (Dormitory), and the Rere-Dorter (Lavatories).

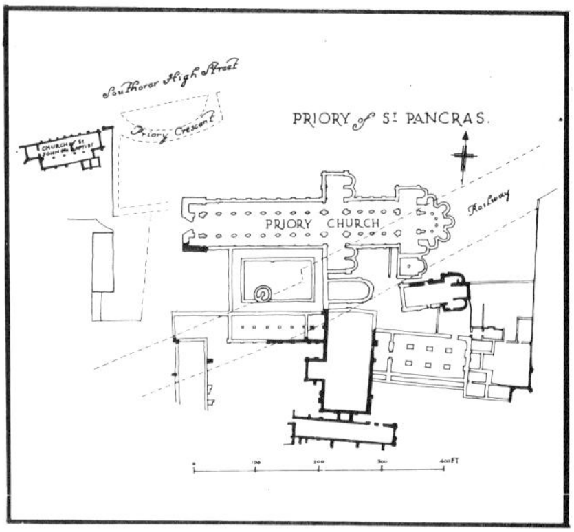

17E Plan of the Priory Precinct.

The fabric of the Priory suffered two severe setbacks to its survival, the first was the Dissolution of the Monasteries ordered by Henry VIII in the 1530s. The second was the construction of the railway through the middle of the enclave in 1845, uncovering the Romanesque tombs of William and Gundreda, which now reside in Southover Parish Church. Next to the Church is the almost intact Priory Gate House, and to the east of the site is the mysterious artificial mound believed by a few to have been the motte of William's first castle.

Relics and drawings of the Priory can be found in the Lewes Living History Centre and at Anne of Cleves House museum nearby.

17G Fitzroy Memorial Library
High Street

This small and fascinating public library was built in memory of Henry Fitzroy, MP and designed by Sir George Gilbert Scott in 1862. He also designed Brighton College Main

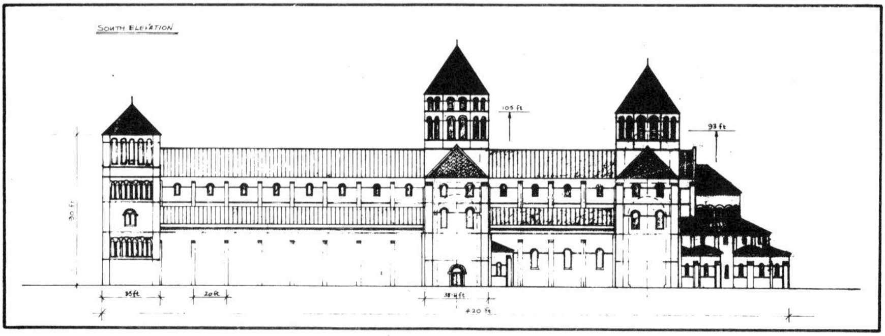

17E Conjectural South Elevation of the Priory, drawing by Andy Gammon and Colin Brent.

School Building (see 8J). Scott was commissioned because he was the most successful architect of his time and an advocate of the Gothic style. The design appears to have been very carefully conceived by Scott: it consists of a two storey block, surmounted by a fleche, fronting a large square toplit library space. It has a symmetrical facade and it is constructed in red brickwork in a modified Italian Gothic style à la Ruskin.

In 1897 necessary repairs altered the appearance of the facade. The diaper patterned brick parapet walls were removed to allow exposure of the eaves. This modification detracts from the stylistic unity of the facade, but appears to greatly increase its charm. By 1955 the building proved too small and the library was moved to another G. G. Scott building nearby. In 1970 the building was under threat of demolition, to be replaced by a shopping development. DoE listing has saved all but the octagonal roof. It is now a private residence.

17H Old County Hall 1808-1812
High Street

In 1808 the Justices of the Peace decided to revive the idea first suggested in 1800 of demolishing the Sessions House built in 1761, and erecting a larger version in a new location. The old Sessions House was a stone quoined, brick structure which had half of its ground floor open, had its courtroom located on the first floor and was surmounted by a small campanile. It stood in the middle of Lewes High Street opposite the White Hart Hotel, on the site of an earlier wooden structure. Commenting on its position astride the town's main highway a Lewes historian in 1795 called it, " . . . a perfect nuisance on account of its very improper situation and a monument to the stupidity of those who fixed it there".

John Johson's 1801 plans to erect a new building on the north side of the road were delayed for seven years due to the threat of invasion by the French during the Napoleonic Wars. Subsquently an Act of Parliament was obtained and work on the project began to progress quickly. By this time the architect John Johnson was 80 and infirm and the responsibility for the project was placed in the hands of a solicitor, William Langridge.

The present structure is not a true representation of the proposed design which was similar in some respects to Johnson's earlier Essex County Hall in Chelmsford. The original scheme was for a ground floor of five bays with an open colonnade, flanked on the left by an office for the Clerk of the Peace, and on the right by a Magistrates Room. The courts were placed at first floor and were double height. A problem arose when it was discovered that the architect had not allowed for the projection of a neighbouring Hatter's shop and as a result the owner had to be paid off for the removal of the obstruction. Later the Committee overseeing the project decided to change and enlarge the original plans. The building was completed externally in 1810, only 18 months after the passing of the Act. The old Sessions House was then sold for £450 to Amon Wilds who later had it removed.

The building has a brick carcase faced with 100 mm thick Portland Stone and adorned with three figures of Wisdom, Justice and Mercy in alto relief made from Coade's durable artificial stone. In 1900 the east end was extended in a similar manner except for the carved ornament which was in Portland Stone rather than Coade Stone, the recipe for which had been sadly lost.

17K The High Street, Lewes

When it was first built in 1853 the County Gaol sat in the fields on the edge of the town. Designed by D. R. Hill, the round arched windows, low towers and machicolations make Lewes Prison, a disquieting yet attractive enclave. Just to the south east stands St. Anne's Crescent, built in the 1870s it is a serene curve of rather opulent Italianate villas located off the main road. Nearby the Greenwich Meridian is acknowledged by a plaque and a mark on the pavement.

17K St. Anne's Church.

From here the main road into the town is fronted by a succession of interesting buildings. The Norman Tower of St. Anne's Church is followed by the Elizabethan front of the Shelley Hotel on the left, and thence to the crisp knapped flintwork of the Grammar School, rebuilt in 1851. Opposite stands St. Anne's House, built in 1719 with five bays and an Ionic porch. The "bottleneck" introducing the mediaeval town

17K Keere Street.

is marked by Keere Street to the south. It is the town's oldest cobbled street and it follows the line of the 13th century Town Wall which becomes visible nearer the Grange. It was here that the Prince Regent, later George IV, is reported to have driven a coach and four downhill for a wager. The timbered 15th century Bookshop stands at the top of Keere Street where a milestone proclaims the distance to Brighthelmstone. Opposite is the 1868 High Victorian Gothic Freemason's Hall, on the site of West Gate. Next lies Pipe Passage, typical of Lewes's network of twittens and on the line of the sentry walk of the old wall. Bull House beside the southern bastion of the Gate housed briefly, radical author of the "Rights of Man", Thomas Paine (1737-1809).

17K St. Michael's Church.

St. Michael's was built probably as the Castle Church. The round Norman Tower of knapped flint supporting a shingled spire, unfortunately, has been covered with pebble dash. The street frontage of knapped, squared and coursed flint dates from 1748, but with later windows.

17K The "Bottleneck".

Amon Wilds built four houses in Castle Place in a terrace sometime before 1811. In 1816 the eminent Palaeontologist Dr. Gideon Mantell, took over No. 3 Castle Place from his partner Dr. Moore who had lived there for some years. Three years later, in 1819, he bought the adjoining house, No. 2 Castle

17K Castle Place,
drawing by Philip Andrews.

Place, from Amon Wilds. Wilds then skilfully converted Nos. 2 and 3 into one residence and it came to be known as Castle Place. The merged house still stands today and is one of the most charming houses in the area. The facade is decorated on its flanks by giant fluted pilasters supporting Ammonite capitals. The "Ammonite order" was originally used by George Dance on the facade of Boydell's Gallery in Pall Mall in 1789 and was probably inspired by the drawings of Battista Piranesi a founding father of Neo-classicism. Thc volutes of the capitals are designed in the form of ammonites resembling the horn of Jupiter Amon in shape. It was a most appropriate order to use on the residence of a distinguished geologist and it was used many times by Amon Henry Wilds who may have been intrigued by the pun on his own name. The delicate wrought iron balustrade to the balcony is in delightful contrast to the heavy Ionic porch and upper cornice. The rusticated piano nobile is surmounted by tall elegant first floor windows with smaller second floor windows above, punctuated by a continuous cill course. The deep cornice is bracketed and supports a stone balustrade, finished at the ends with a capping of shell ornamentation.

In front of the Barbican sits Bartholomew House 1815, possibly by Wilds, and a fine example of black mathematical tiles. On the right hand side is Barbican House, a timber framed building with an 18th century modernised exterior, which was once the home of Thomas Read Kemp. The somewhat incongruous, but nevertheless, good redbrick Town Hall was designed by Samuel Denman

17K Lewes from the Cliffe.

of Brighton in 1893 and built on the site of the Star Inn whose cellars confined seventeen protestant martyrs.

Further down School Hill reveals mathematical tiling in various guises. There is a delightful twin doorway arrangement at "Patissons" restaurant on the left and a most imposing portico graces Lewes House opposite. The Fitzroy Library now encircled by new development turns the corner into Friars Walk. The High Street ends with the bridge link to the mediaeval commercial suburb of the Cliffs where 19th century warehouses hark back to the once thriving river trade.

17K Portico at Lewes House.

17L The Old Needlemakers
West Street

The Old Needlemakers was built in the 1820s as Broad's Candle Factory. Before lying derelict for many years it also served as a surgical needle factory, a builder's merchants and a potter's store. In the 1970s Lewes District Council bought the property in order to clear the site and expand West Street car park. Pressure from local conservationists blocked this proposal and prepared the way for an ideas competition. The complex was sold to Lewes Workspace Ltd. owned jointly by Gillian Harwood and Phillip Lancashire. They designed a scheme with two storeys of studios for small businesses above two storeys of craft workshops.

The conversion, completed in September 1985, incorporates more retail space on the lower floors reflecting local demand for such units and a most attractive cafe which specialises in refreshments for visitors. The top half of the existing building had to be completely rebuilt. The design of the new structure, however, has been sensitively and imaginatively carried out in timber complementing the flitch beams which support the first floor. This is a fine example of the re-use of an obsolete industrial building in the centre of a town.

17N Clevedown, Elderly Persons Housing
Brighton Road

This imaginative arrangement of flats sponsored by the local Housing Association was designed for the ambulant disabled. It has been handled with a care and sensitivity which responds both to its environs and its occupants.

The scheme was designed by the Michael Blee Whittaker Partnership (see 10L, 15G) who developed a plan generated by the existence of a mature garden once attached to an Edwardian house. This serves as a focus for the residential community accommodated in five double-fronted pavilions with a dual aspect. Emphasis is given to the introverted nature of the scheme whilst the contours of the site are reflected in the arc of pavilions as they cascade gently down the slope. The effect is the attainment of a sequence of spaces similar in essence to those found around the town.

The scheme comprises seventy warden assisted sheltered units which have their own identity inside as well as on the facade. Long institutional corridors are avoided and a central common space is provided within each block from where entry can be gained to individual flats and the time of day passed agreeably with neighbours. Links between the blocks offer little protection from the elements, but allow a choice of meandering routes through the garden. The brief has no provision for wheelchair disabled. Spare bedrooms are provided for family visitors in an adjacent existing stable block.

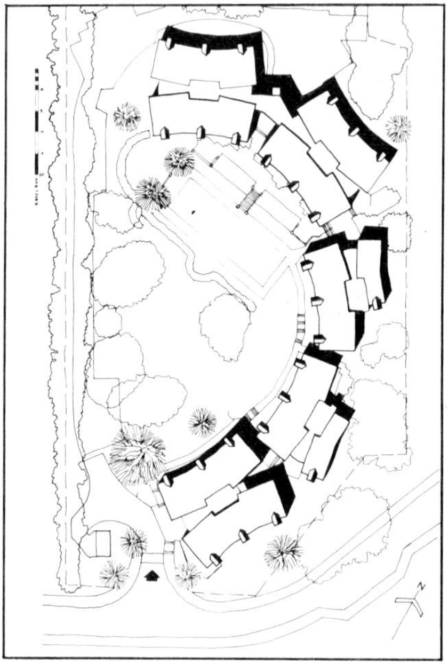

17N Plan of Clevedown.

17P Southover Grange
Southover Road

The Grange is an outstanding example of an Elizabethan Manor House. It was commissioned in 1572 by William Newton, reputed to be a cousin of Sir Isaac Newton of Cheshire, and it bears his initials and coat of arms on the main fireplace. The building has a terraced frontage with gables surmounted by an array of handsome brick chimney stacks. The roof is largely of Horsham stone and handmade clay tiles and the walls are constructed from Caen stone taken from the Priory which had been razed to the ground forty years earlier.

Many alterations have been undertaken since 1572; the oak panelled outer hall, which has two stone mullioned windows, dates from 1873 and was originally an open court. The chestnut roof timbers used throughout the house are original, but there is only one original staircase and that is in the north wing.

17P Southover Grange.

The most distinguished interior space is the 21 foot high main hall, panelled in oak up to 8 feet and lit by stone mullioned windows, glazed with painted glass.

Much of the charm of the building is derived from its asymmetrical form and its relationship to a very beautiful garden. Some claim that its attraction is enhanced by its reputation for being haunted and blighted by a traditional curse.

17Q Waterloo Place Development.

17Q Waterloo Place Development

This housing scheme on the corner of Little East Street and North Street was designed by Paul Hodgkins Associates and completed in 1981. The scheme derives its name from the earlier buildings which stood on the site and which were erected to commemorate the Battle of Waterloo. The "Iron Duke" is depicted on the weather vane fixed on the top of the pyramidal roof of the corner building.

The development comprises 22 three-person flats, 19 two-person flats and 8 family houses. The ground floor units for disabled residents are smaller than those above and the first floor oversails it, producing a pronounced jetty, a feature reminiscent of mediaeval building forms.

Two new public spaces have been created: Waterloo Place and the area between North Street and Wellington Street. They are a response to the mediaeval pattern of Lewes which is about links between buildings rather than formal public open spaces. The facades are constructed in Rudgewick Stock bricks, set off with reconstituted stone lintols and padstones or, on the larger units, black brick cills, quoins, arches and string courses, which contrast with the tonal qualities of the neighbouring terrace.

18 SHOREHAM

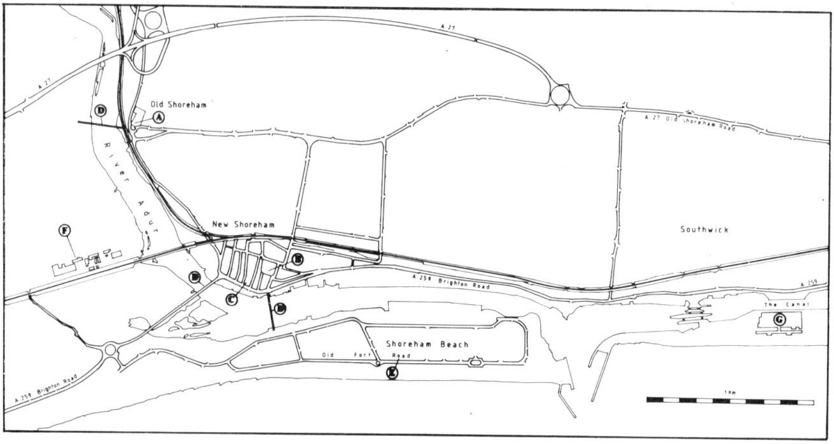

Shoreham, which is situated seven miles west of Brighton, was originally two settlements of different date now merged by building into one. Old Shoreham was the original Saxon village and port until 1100 AD when, due to the river Adur silting up, it became necessary to move it southwards. The area round the Church of St. Nicholas is all that remains of this original settlement. New Shoreham was built by the Normans. The town was always at the mercy of the shifting course of the river which swept away much of the area south of the High Street. This included a Carmelite Priory which had strong links with the Church of St. Mary. Shoreham still possesses two magnificent churches and an interesting 12th century storehouse. Inigo Jones was Shoreham's Member of Parliament in 1620, but sadly never its architect.

Further silting up of the Adur in late mediaeval times intensified Shoreham's activity as a port once the river became no longer navigable as far as Bramber. In the 18th century Shoreham became a busy shipbuilding town benefitting from the decline of Brighton as a port and gradually it attracted more coastal traffic, particularly coal for Brighton. The building of the basin to the east at Portslade in 1854 aided its expansion. In the late 19th and early 20th centuries the locked basin provided an ideal site for a large gas works (now demolished) and for a power station, whose younger partner still dominates the coastline. The two others, built by the Borough of Brighton have been demolished.

Across the Adur estuary is the fine prospect of Lancing College designed by R. C. Carpenter and founded in 1848 by Nathaniel Woodward, then curate of New Shoreham.

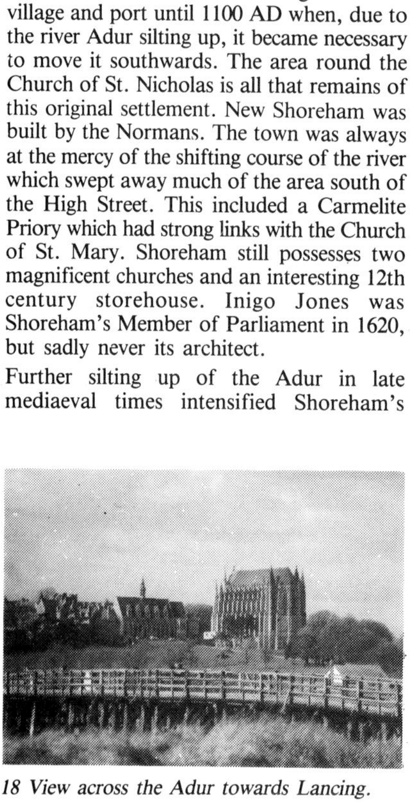

18 View across the Adur towards Lancing.

18A St. Nicholas's Church, Old Shoreham
The original Saxon church was built during the 10th century and now constitutes the nave and tower crossing of the present structure. The location of the Saxon tower can be traced at the west end of the nave. The Saxon entrance is on the north face and is blocked up. The church was extensively reconstructed by the Normans in 1140, when its form was changed from a linear one with tower entrance, nave and chancel, to a cruciform configuration with a new tower, a chancel with an aspidal end, and transepts with chapels at the east end. The impression is one of an important Norman village church. This is perhaps partly due to the amount of restoration work carried out in the 1840s. The other Norman parts are a blocked up doorway

18A St. Nicholas's Church, Old Shoreham.

on the north wall of the nave, the entrance door in the south transept, the tower, the tower arches and a tie beam at the east end of the nave. The interior of the church is dominated by the exuberantly carved Norman arches.

During the 14th century the Norman chancel and transept chapels were demolished and replaced by an early English chancel, greater in length and with a square east end. Next to the north transpet was a chapel now long since demolished. There is a 13th century carved tie beam in the chancel and a painted ceiling of Victorian date.

The church owes its present condition largely to J. M. Neale and J. C. Buckler and the Cambridge Camden Society. In the 1840s they carried out substantial repairs and much restoration which Pevsner finds questionable in parts. At the northern end of the graveyard are several examples of war graves designed by Lutyens.

18B St. Mary De Haura, New Shoreham

St. Mary of the Harbour is one of the leading fifty non-cathedral greater churches in the country according to John Harvey, an acclaimed authority on English church architecture. It was built between 1100 and 1225 and it is an important example of the transition from Norman to Gothic church building. The church today is only half its original length. The ruins of the original south-west corner of the nave can still be seen in the churchyard. Only one bay of the old nave remains as the rest eventually collapsed after destruction by either a French raid in 1628 or by parliamentary forces in the Civil War. The present church is the remaining bay of the nave, the tower crossing and transepts, which are Norman, and the choir, which is transitional. Originally the church had a chancel with an apsidal end and transeptal chapels as at Old Shoreham (18A). Between 1180-1225 the transitional additions were built,

18B St. Mary de Haura.

including the top level of the tower, the aisles, the choir and the vaulting. The chancel and chapels were replaced by a much finer structure, the choir with aisles, five bays and a square east end. And it is this addition which is of outstanding interest in New Shoreham as it catches the moment of change in the transition from Norman to Gothic architecture. The bays and arches are in two sets. The north side has alternate solid round and octagonal columns, Norman in essence. They carry decorated slightly pointed arches which are richly carved. The south side is first stage Gothic with the shafts of the columns from floor to vaulting. The tower also reflects change where the second stage uses visually lighter pointed arches over first stage round arches.

18B St. Mary de Haura from the Adur Estuary.

18C The Marlipins

The Marlipins is situated on the north side of the High Street. It appears that it has always been a two-storeyed store and it is of a similar age to the earlier parts of St. Mary's Church (18B). It may have been the custom house originally. There is little evidence of Norman work and apart from one 12th century window on the east side the building is dominated by its early 14th century additions. They include the chequerboard front facade and its restored two higher windows. This south facade is a pattern of Caen stone and flints arranged in a precise manner, which perhaps helps to verify its early use as an important secular building to the busy port. Since the 14th century the building has been used mainly for storage purposes, probably for wines and beers. In the 19th century it was used as a toy shop and today the building serves as a museum of local history and is the source of much interesting material about the buildings and the area.

18C The Marlipins.

18D The Bridges of Shoreham

The first recorded building of a bridge across the Adur at Shoreham followed the passing of an Act of Parliament in 1781. It was for the construction of a timber bridge at Old

18D The Old Bridge.

Shoreham, as it appears that the ferry crossing was becoming increasingly hazardous and the road busier, partly due to traffic between Brighton and new resorts west of the Adur. There were earlier bridges across the Adur going back to the Roman occupation, but they were sited to the north, at Bramber or Botolphs as part of the east-west Roman highway. Later bridges were built there, possibly replacing Roman models.

Before the building of the Old Shoreham bridge there were two ferries in use. The Old Shoreham Ferry was mentioned in a Parliamentary Survey of Old Shoreham Manor dated 1651. The other ferry, at Ropetackle at the west end of the coast road, now Shoreham High Street, connected with a wharf across the water serving the upper Lancing Road and goes back to mediaeval times.

The 1781 bridge was in use until 1971 when it was replaced by a box girder structure. The first Norfolk Bridge just south of Ropetackle was opened in 1833. It was an interesting suspension structure supported by two arched pylons built in ashlar. The design was by W. Tierney Clarke, who was also the architect for Hammersmith Bridge where the iron work was conceived by Samuel Brown, originator of the Chain Pier at Brighton, 1823. Brown worked with Telford and then Brunel who incorporated some of his ideas in their new bridge designs.

A third ferry came into use to serve Shoreham Beach until a footbridge was opened in 1921. Horses and carts were able to make the crossing at a ford at low tide.

The second Norfolk bridge, built in 1922-23, was a crude replacement of the first and has itself been replaced by a wider structure in concrete constructed alongside it and completed in 1987.

18F Shoreham Airport.

18E Shoreham Beach
The shingle beach was discovered by an enchanted theatrical profession in the very late 1800s, a large number of whom made it their seaside residential area. Bungalow Town became a seaside retreat for Music Hall, Variety theatre entertainers and serious actors, as well as impresarios, theatre proprietors and sportsmen. A number of bungalows were built, many of them based on the utilisation of redundant railway stock of the then London South Coast Railway. Their construction was simply a concrete raft, two carriages to provide the basic accommodation with a roof spanning the gap, creating a large living space. A chapel of ease, several shops, a pub and a film studio were also built. Bungalow Town was attractive to pioneers of the film industry in its early days. A number of small film companies worked at Shoreham Beach from before the First World War until the thirties. The Second World War brought Bungalow Town to an end. In 1940 the residents were given 48 hours to leave and the army destroyed almost all of the bungalows as a security measure in case of invasion. There are now only two recognisable examples left, one of which has undergone a thorough restoration including the LSCR Livery. The last remnants of the unique colony remain amongst the suburban residential development which has grown since its demise.

18C Shoreham Beach.

18F Shoreham Airport
Shoreham is the oldest working commercial airport in existence. It became one of the first flying fields in the country in 1910 when Harold Pifford, a former pupil of Lancing College, took off in this 40 hp Shoreham built biplane. In 1911 the first cargo flight in Britain was undertaken when a box of Osram lamps was flown from Shoreham to Hove. The following year Avros moved their depot to Shoreham where they assembled and tested their planes, utilising the estuary for sea trials. The airport was purchased by the boroughs of Brighton, Hove and Worthing in 1930 in order to establish a municipal airport for the three towns. A terminal building and hangar were built between 1934 and 1938. The architect chosen to design the terminal

18F Shoreham Airport.

building was R. Stavers Tiltman. He was also responsible for building a chain of pubs in Sussex and like Oliver Hill he seemed able to switch readily from Sussex vernacular or Georgian style for pubs, to a popular cognate of the international white architecture for airports. Unacceptable at the time to the cognoscenti of CIAM and the MARS group, the terminal building with its central control tower has a dash of Art Deco in its motifs and a pronounced symmetry in its layout and massing. However, it seems to have an enduring quality about it and its concrete construction has worn well over the years. During the Second World War the airport was used as a fighter base and was not returned to commercial use until 1951.

Only in the last five years has Shoreham had an all weather capacity runway. This has restricted its development and much to the relief, no doubt, of the occupants of nearby houses, it remains a charming reminder of the early days of flying.

18G Shoreham 'B' Power Station

Shoreham 'B' was first conceived in the early 40s to fulfill the need for a large modern installation to supply electricity for the south-east area. It was built in 1947-48, after the electricity supply industry was nationalised, with a capacity of 342 MW to be fed into the national grid. The designer consulting was architect G. H. Somerset and the engineer, Price Jones. The new plant was housed in a building which is extremely large and monumental and acknowledges the achievement of Sir Giles Gilbert Scott at Battersea, 1929-55. Sited on the eastern arm of Shoreham Harbour this essay in monolithic symbolism is impressive. Whether its imagery is more appropriate than that of a technologically innovative design, as demonstrated at Dunston Co. Durham a decade earlier, is a matter for conjecture or even taste.

This formidable construction required 6,000 reinforced concrete driven piles down to depths of 15 metres to support the basement floor. 15 million bricks were required for the complete structure. Silver grey and bronze facing bricks were selected by the architect to blend with the natural tones of the surrounding beach, and care was taken to ensure consistency in the design elements.

The massive dimensions of the building are shown in the Turbine Room, which is 255 metres long, 18 metres wide and 24 metres high; the Boiler Room, which is 270 metres long, 30 metres wide and 35 metres high; and the chimneys which are 100 metres high and faced in fluted concrete. There is a cable tunnel under the harbour, 27 metres below ground and 3 metres in diameter.

The harbour was enlarged and improved by Sir William Halcrow and Partners for the Central Electricity Authority. It was completed in 1957 and was then able to accommodate vessels of 4,500 tonnes. The consumption of the plant is 300 tonnes of coal per hour.

18G Shoreham 'B' Power Station.

INDEX OF PEOPLE

INDEX OF PLACES

House fronts in Montpelier Road by Amon Henry Wilds.

BOOKS FOR FURTHER READING

Colin Brent	'Historic Lewes'. Lewes Town Council, 1985. An excellent pocket guide to Lewes.
Anthony Dale	'Fashionable Brighton 1820-1860' Oriel Press 1967 (1947). Packed with detailed information, the first account of the work of Busby and the Wilds.
Anthony Dale	'About Brighton'. The Regency Society of Brighton and Hove, 1951. A useful pocket book.
Sue Farrant	'Georgian Brighton 1740-1820'. University of Sussex Centre for Continuing Education, 1980. A detailed account of the growth of Brighton as a resort.
Sue Farrant with K. Fosey and A. Peasgood	'The Growth of Brighton and Hove, 1840-1939. University of Sussex Centre for Continuing Education, 1981. The development of modern Brighton.
Edmund M. Gilbert	'Brighton, An Ocean's Bauble'. Flare Books 1975 (1954). An excellent general history of Brighton.
H. S. Goodhart-Rendel	'The Churches of Brighton and Hove'. Architectural Review, 1918, Aug. Sept. Oct.
Judy Middleton	'The History of Hove', Phillimore, 1979. A general history of Hove.
Clifford Musgrave	'Life in Brighton'. Archon Books, 1970. A very full account of the history of Brighton.
Ian Nairn and Nikolaus pevsner	'The Buildings of England: Sussex'. Penguin Books, 1965. Invaluable, irritating, not always accurate.
Gordon Somerville	'Hove's Architectural Heritage'. Opus, 1986. A description of Hove's conservation areas.
Anthony Wagner and Antony Dale	'The Wagners of Brighton', Phillimore 1983. A very detailed history of the family which built so many of Brighton's churches.

ABOUT THE AUTHORS

This guide has been researched and written by Clive Atkinson, David Matthews, Andrew Savile, Robert Tunna and Tim Weighill, final year students in the School of Architecture and Interior Design of Brighton Polytechnic. Ken Macdonald and David Robson, Diploma Course lecturers in the School of Architecture, supervised the project and acted as general editors. Sue Farrant, a senior lecturer at Brighton Polytechnic whose research interests include the history and architecture of seaside resorts and who has published extensively on the history of Brighton, has acted as joint editor and special adviser.

The authors wish to thank Glen Patching and Jean Middleton of Brighton Polytechnic, Bernard Stonestreet of the SE Region of the RIBA and Sue Hoekstra for their help and encouragement. The project was greatly assisted by a grant from the John and Heather Lomax Student Prize, and special thanks are due to John Lomax who was Head of the School of Architecture from 1967 to 1984.